APOCALYPSE THEN AND NOW

APOCALYPSE THEN AND NOW

A Companion to the Book of Revelation

ROLAND J. FALEY

PAULIST PRESS
New York ◆ Mahwah, N.J.

Cover design by Nick Markell

Cover illustration: from a woodcut of Albrecht Durer, *Four Horsemen of the Apocalypse,* used with permission of the Dover Pictorial Archive series, Dover Publications, Inc. (31 E. Second Street; Mineola, N.Y. 11501).

Map, "The Seven Lampstands Are the Seven Churches" © 1999, Ted Leavenworth, Goodnews Christian Ministry.

Map design by Frank Sabatté, C.S.P.

Scripture selections are taken from the New American Bible with Revised New Testament Copyright © 1986, 1970 by the Confraternity of Christian Doctrine, 3211 Fourth Street, N.E., Washington, D.C. 20017-1194 and are used by license of the copyright owner. All rights reserved. No part of the New American Bible may be reproduced in any form without permission in writing from the copyright owner.

Library of Congress Cataloging-in-Publication Data

Faley, Roland J. (Roland James), 1930–
    Apocalypse then and now : a companion to the book of Revelation / by Roland J. Faley.
      p. cm.
    Includes bibliographical references and index.
    ISBN 0-8091-3895-6 (alk. paper)
    1. Bible. N.T. Revelation Commentaries. I. Title.
BS2825.3 .F27 1999
228′.077–dc21

                                                    99–34678
                                                      CIP

Published by Paulist Press
997 Macarthur Boulevard
Mahwah, New Jersey 07430

www.paulistpress.com

Printed and bound in the
United States of America

CONTENTS

To my sister
Sally

Strong and graceful and
cheerful about the future
—Proverbs 31:25

INTRODUCTION

Chiliasm. A word that is clearly not part of our modern vocabulary. Bearing a distinctly religious connotation, it speaks of a thousand-year reign of Christ, during which evil is suppressed, as a preface to "the end of the world." The thousand years has had a variety of interpretations in the history of Christianity. In the light of a time sequence mentioned in the Book of Revelation, many people identified the beginning of this final period with the year A.D. 1000. The first thousand years of the Christian era had seen the conflict between good and evil in very vivid historical terms. With the collapse of the Roman Empire, the rise to power of the northern *barbari* and the emergence of what is rather inaccurately termed the Holy Roman Empire, the conflict between Augustine's City of God and the City of Man had moved to the forefront. It was now time for the beginning of the end. What Revelation had described as the thousand-year period during which good would come to the fore while the forces of evil remained chained seemed to loom on the horizon. The year 1000 was the beginning of the end. The millennium combined an historical eschatology (the earthly reign of Christ) with an apocalyptic one, centering on the "end of the world" (cosmic upheaval, final battle). It was seen as a moment of immense transition and was charged with frightening, even terrifying features. There was to be a partial or first resurrection of the dead. And it all loomed large as the year A.D. 1000 approached. The moral message was clear enough: Be prepared and your chances are reasonably good. Be unprepared and live—or die—with the consequences.

We have now reached the end of the second millennium of the Christian era, and while the climate is considerably more tranquil and expectations more modest, there is a renewed interest in that little known or understood book of the Bible known as Apocalypse or Revelation—the book that in its mysterious makeup has triggered so much speculation in the course of history.

Apocalypse Then and Now is a modest attempt to interpret Revelation and help to remove the aura of mystery that envelops it. My interest in writing this book was partly chiliastic or millennium-oriented. Since I had never taught a New Testament course on Revelation, I thought that such might be appropriate before the end of my teaching days, which will probably coincide approximately with the turn of the century. A certain sense of drama convinced me that a reverent salute to the Bible's final book might fittingly mark the end of a teaching career.

The venture proved extremely interesting. There is no better test of one's understanding of the Old Testament than by "decoding" the images and symbols with which Revelation abounds. Revelation is, moreover, a book of immense hope, supported by the certainty of faith. Good and evil are as central to its message as are reward and punishment. It was written at a time of intense persecution, yet written with a fearless spirit. Regardless of how great and powerful the forces of evil, embodied above all in imperial Rome, they were no match for the enthroned God and his Christ. And while evil might have its day, the last word had not yet been spoken. Ultimately glory and honor belong to the One seated on the throne and to the Lamb. And that praise will be offered by those who have weathered the storm of the present life.

As I state clearly in the commentary sections of this book, for the Christian of today, the end time is already with us. While it still moves inexorably to its conclusion, it is not simply looming on the horizon. We are living it now. To illustrate the point, the book of Daniel serves us well; no book of the Bible is more strongly eschatological, composed about one hundred and fifty years before the Christian era. It speaks of the final days in vivid apocalyptic terms. The New Testament authors see the teaching of Daniel fulfilled in the coming of Christ. In his infancy narrative, Luke draws on Daniel's visions, the angelic messenger Gabriel, and the "seventy weeks" which were to predate the reconsecration of the temple—all to present the end time converging in the person of Christ.

As Christians who now live in the final era, the Book of Revelation should have meaning for us. Therefore, a considerable part of the present study is dedicated to the work's significance today. In addition to the text and commentary, I have added at the end of each section a reflection and application that attempt to bring the text to life for our times.

While considering the needs of the individual reader, who will, I hope, find the book a spiritual and intellectual stimulus, I have kept in mind as well the needs of parish or community study groups, who find the study of the Bible a source of spiritual growth. The text is also geared to the study of Revelation in an academic setting. To help spark reflection or discussion, I have included a series of points at the conclusion of each section; these questions converge around issues related to the chapter itself.

I am truly indebted to many people who, throughout these many years as I have attempted to explain God's Word, have been so encouraging and affirming. I am particularly grateful to my Franciscan confreres who have endured and supported me in a variety of ways over the years. Special mention must be made of Thérèse and Adam Zaid for their valuable and amicable assistance in preparing this work for publication.

THE BOOK OF REVELATION

Our journey begins on the Aegean island of Patmos, a Roman penal colony. It is from there that the exiled John writes to seven churches. As a visionary he depicts the events of the present and of the future in highly symbolic terms. This veiled type of language, known as *apocalyptic,* draws on themes of the Old and New Testaments to describe the final summing up of salvation history. We date the Book of Revelation toward the end of the first century of the Christian era, during the reign of the emperor Domitian (81–96). There had been by this time a limited persecution of Christians, but nothing on the scale to which the author refers when looking at the approaching end-time disaster. Evil will have its day, as the book plainly indicates, but it will be followed by the era of Christ's triumph and the definitive overthrow of the evil one. Hence, this is a book of shadow and light, "bad news and good news," disaster and vindication.

POLITICO-HISTORICAL SCENE

Asia Minor saw a large influx of Jews and Christians in the period following the Roman destruction of Jerusalem. But the antagonism between church and synagogue had by this time become quite pronounced. In the earliest stages, the infant church, even with its distinctive claims, was seen as another Jewish sect, but with the continued emphasis on Jesus as the Messiah, an eventual split became inevitable. The Christians certainly did not have a high profile in Asia Minor; their members were mostly of the lower classes, whereas the Jews were much more respected by the Romans and the ruling class. As time passed, Christians were seen as *personae non gratae* by Jews and Gentiles alike.

There is little doubt that one of the main bones of contention between Romans and Christians centered on emperor worship. The attempt to divinize the emperor goes back to the time of Alexander the Great; it reaches its apogee in the time of Nero (54–68) and continued in the time of Domitian (81–96). It was stringently enforced in Domitian's time, with reprisals against those who refused to acquiesce. This ongoing conflict was the backdrop against which Revelation was written.

A PASTORAL LETTER

The letter was to be read publicly in a liturgical setting. It is clear that the audiences were congregations known personally to the author, communities that he wished to encourage. There is no indication that Revelation was seen as the last book of the Bible, or for that matter, even as a book. If we can imagine the destinaries of the letter to be, to a considerable extent, Christians of a Jewish background, then the imagery used would not have been unfamiliar. The letter is prophetic (1:3) in the sense that it interprets the meaning of actual events and ties them in with the total vision of God's saving plan. All of this is done within the framework of Christ's first and second coming. When John speaks of his visions, he is obviously speaking of supernatural experiences, but he "fleshes" this out with pictures, images, and ideas drawn from his own knowledge and experience.

THE AUTHOR

We can best identify him as the prophet John, the seer John, or John of Patmos. He makes no claim to being one of the twelve (21:14) and recounts nothing from the earthly life of Jesus. He is certainly to be distinguished from the John of the Johannine literature in terms of theological outlook, style, and vocabulary. He seems to have known Aramaic or Hebrew better than Greek, since his writing is rough and full of semitisms. If we can come to any determination, it would be that he was a Palestinian Jewish

Christian who emigrated to Asia Minor some time after the year 70.

THE GENRE: APOCALYPTIC

The book is clearly eschatological, wholly centered on the end time. God is the end of history, just as he was its beginning; hence final intervention is a given. It should be seen as an act of covenant love as well as one of judgment, since it providentially brings the whole process of salvation to its determined end. But the end time still remains veiled in mystery, and it is precisely there that the language of apocalyptic enters. Since the author does not know precisely what form the end will take, he draws on images and symbols, sometimes jarring and disjointed and frequently taken from the Old Testament, to make his point. Examples of this genre are found in the Old Testament itself, especially in the Book of Daniel and the "little apocalypse" of Isaiah (cc. 24–27). Apocalyptic literature is engaging, since it needs to be "decoded" while at the same time remaining shrouded in mystery.

And this leads to another interesting purpose of this genre in first-century Christianity. It provided the veiled language that enabled Christians to speak of actual or impending historical events. This meant that the message of Revelation was not directly accessible to all, least of all to Roman oppressors. It had to be "decoded," a feat best accomplished by those familiar with the Hebrew scriptures and early Christian imagery. Thus apocalyptic language served as something of a "safety net" for early believers.

Apocalyptic has captured the minds of Christian interpreters throughout the centuries, something especially true in the case of Revelation. At various times, Protestants have seen the great beast as the Roman papacy, and Catholics have interpreted the whole evil empire in terms of Martin Luther's Reformation. The best procedure, and the one adopted here, is to determine the original meaning and then raise questions about its meaning today. There is no question that the author of Revelation expected the end to come soon and never envisioned a church now beginning its third millennium of life. This is but one of the limitations of inspiration as coming from a human author, who despite his special gifts remains very much a human being. It is within that framework that the interpreter must search for the fundamental message.

STRUCTURE OF THE BOOK OF REVELATION

Part I: Letters to the churches of Asia (1:1–3:22)
The destinary churches are Ephesus, Smyrna, Pergamum, Thyatira, Sardis, Philadelphia, and Laodicea.

Part II: Judgment on the Evil Empire (4:1–18:24)
This includes the seven Seals, Trumpets, Bowls, and Plagues, which herald the destruction of the power of evil.

Part III: Final Redemption—The New Creation (19:1–22:5)

Part IV: Epilogue (22:6–21)

BOOK OF REVELATION OUTLINE

THE SEVEN CHURCHES *(cc. 1–3)*

Ephesus	Smyrna	Pergamum	Thyatira	Sardis	Philadelphia	Laodicea

HONOR TO THE THRONE (GOD) AND THE LAMB *(cc. 4–5)*

THE SEVEN SEALS *(c. 6)*

War	Violence	Famine	Death	Martyrdom	Earthquake	Silence 8:1

SEALING OF THE ELECT *(c. 7)*

THE SEVEN TRUMPETS *(cc. 8–9) (11:15–19)*

Fire	Sea	Bitter Water	Falling Stars	Locusts	Horses	Glory

INTERVAL: Scroll, Measuring Rod, Trees, Lampstand *(cc. 10–11)*

Conflict *(c. 12)* ➤➤ **Beasts** *(c. 13)* ➤➤

SEVEN HARBINGERS OF FATE *(c. 14)*

ANGEL I	ANGEL II	ANGEL III	SON OF MAN	ANGEL IV	ANGEL V	ANGEL VI
Judgment	Fallen Babylon	Punishment	Harvester	Herald of Doom	Harvester	Final Recompense

APPEARANCE OF THE SEVEN ANGELS WITH SEVEN BOWLS *(c. 15)*

THE SEVEN BOWLS *(c. 16)*

Sores	Bloody Sea	Bloody River	Burns	Darkness	Invasion	Earthquake

THE FALL OF BABYLON, THE GREAT HARLOT *(cc. 17–18)*

SEVEN FINAL EVENTS *(cc. 19–22)*

Lamb's Feast	Last Battle	Binding of Satan	The Millennium	Defeat of Gog and Magog	Last Judgment	New Jerusalem

9

THE SEVEN LAMPSTANDS
ARE THE SEVEN CHURCHES

THE SEVEN LAMPSTANDS ARE THE SEVEN CHURCHES OF REVELATION 2-3

10

I. LETTERS TO THE CHURCHES OF ASIA (1:1–3:22)

Ephesus, Smyrna, Pergamum, Thyatira, Sardis, Philadelphia, and Laodicea

The first three chapters of the Book of Revelation constitute a unit. The message, the messenger, the destinaries, and the situation of the churches make up a unified structure, even though the situation in each of the churches is distinct.

PROLOGUE (1:1–3)

1:1 **The revelation of Jesus Christ, which God gave to him, to show his servants what must happen soon. He made it known by sending his angel to his servant John,**

1:2 **who gives witness to the word of God and to the testimony of Jesus Christ by reporting what he saw.**

1:3 **Blessed is the one who reads aloud and blessed are those who listen to this prophetic message and heed what is written in it, for the appointed time is near.**

GREETINGS TO THE CHURCHES OF ASIA (1:4–8)

Greeting

1:4 John, to the seven churches in Asia: grace to you and peace from him who is and who was and who is to come, and from the seven spirits before his throne,

1:5 and from Jesus Christ, the faithful witness, the firstborn of the dead and ruler of the kings of the earth. To him who loves us and has freed us from our sins by his blood,

1:6 who has made us into a kingdom, priests for his God and Father, to him be glory and power forever [and ever]. Amen.

1:7 Behold, he is coming amid the clouds,
and every eye will see him,
even those who pierced him.
All the peoples of the earth will lament him.
Yes. Amen.

1:8 "I am the Alpha and the Omega," says the Lord God, "the one who is and who was and who is to come, the almighty."

Prologue (1:1–3)

The scenario presents us with a sequence of persons: God, Christ, the angel and John; Christ, as the bearer of the revelation (Gr.: apokalupsis), *is placed in bold relief. Christ's position is unique; he is not simply another link in the chain. The revelation is defined in him, to whom the Father has committed it, and it turns on events that are soon to take place.* Revelation of Jesus Christ *(v. 1): Is the genitive subjective or objective, that is, a revelation from Jesus Christ or a revelation about him? The context, which deals with the message's transmission, points to its being subjective, that is, a message from Jesus Christ.*

God, not Christ, is the ultimate source of revelation (v. 1). The Word is mediated through Christ, a truth which is applicable to the whole of the New Testament. It is the God who becomes one with us and dies for us in Jesus who stands at the heart of Revelation. The angel is secondary and transient, enjoying no subliminal status. He is a messenger, as in Luke 1, not a being to be exalted (Col 2:18). The author gives a twofold witness, first to the truth as having been received from God and second to Jesus

Christ, who has communicated it (v. 2). Thus there can be no doubt about the fact that this revelation is wrapped in divine certitude. Blessings *(v. 3): Are given to the lector and the hearers. In Hebrew thought, this is much more than a wish or an augury; a blessing has an inherent power, seen very clearly in the story of Jacob and Esau (Gn 27). A blessing declares a fact, much as in the simple statement, "I forgive you."*

For the appointed time is near *(v. 3): It is this note of urgency that will characterize the whole of Revelation. What are we to say about this expectation? Was the author mistaken? Was the early church incorrect in its chronology? The answer is an unequivocal "Yes"; to say otherwise would only make us ingenuous in bending the data. But we should not lose that important sense of urgency, the sense that our generation is the only generation that is present to* us, *at this time. It is not for us to determine the "day or hour" (Mk 13:32), but one cannot forget the fact that every generation, like every individual, has a very clearly determined and limited period of time in which to accomplish God's work.*

The Greeting (vv. 4–8)

The senders are four: John, God, Christ, and the "seven spirits." John, the writer and prophet, is evidently known to the seven churches. The seven spirits: *These are angelic spirits attendant upon the throne of God (3:1; 4:9; 5:6; Ps 104:4; Heb 1:7, 14).* The one who is and who was and who is to come: *God himself, who has an overarching timelessness, eternal but with a determined future.* Jesus Christ: *Jesus is given his full messianic title (Christ–Christos–Messiah), but by this time the term* Christ *has already become a surname for Jesus.*

Jesus is designated as:

• The faithful witness *(v. 5). This is a new title as applied to Christ. But the term is well chosen in as much as the recipients of the letters are witnessing to their faith under duress. Jesus was faithful in attesting to the truth of his own mission even in the face of adversity, through his trial up to the moment of his death (Jn 18:33–19:16; 1 Tim 6:13).*

• Firstborn of the dead *(v. 5; Col 1:18). This addresses the hopes of those who had suffered martyrdom. Jesus holds a priority as the first to rise and the life-giver for those who will follow him. The title also keeps the eschatological focus; the present audience is living in the last days.*

• Ruler of the kings of the earth *(v. 5), a title accorded the Roman emperor and here given to Jesus. It underscores his universal sovereignty.*

Doxology (vv. 5–6): *Christ has primacy and centrality in the hymn of praise. The letter begins with him as a point of origin and recipient of praise. The reason for this is clear: It is Christ who has redeemed us in love.*

Kingdom, priests for our God (v. 6): *The scriptural reference here is Exodus 19:6, "a kingdom of priests, a holy nation." In Revelation, the overarching supremacy of God receives its visible and concrete expression in the community, thus making it a kingdom. In its role of mediating the reconciliation achieved in Christ to the world, the community is priestly. Christ, the anointed one, has a threefold mission—which is continued in the church—that of king, prophet, and priest. Christ is sovereign (king), enunciates God's Word (prophet), and mediates God's love (priest). In this developing Christology, which undoubtedly reflects liturgical use, the Father and Christ are given equal, even if subordinate, recognition.*

In the concluding apotheosis on Christ and God, there are shades of Daniel (7:13) and Zechariah (12:10). It is the apocalyptic son of Man, a frequent designation for Christ in the Gospel tradition, who comes on the clouds of heaven. In Daniel, this represents the new renewed humanity, the holy ones of God, and therefore has a collective sense. In the New Testament this notion is concretized in the person of Christ. The pierced one in Zechariah is surrounded by a mourning Jerusalem, which has unjustly run him through. The grieving equals that for Josiah, who died at Megiddo (Zec 12:11). But the identity of the one mourned remains unclear in the Zechariah text. In Revelation, it clearly refers to Christ and his persecutors, and it takes on a universal sense as "all the peoples of the earth" lament him as an expression of conversion. Behind the son of Man stands God, with his eternal character underscored (Alpha and Omega) and his future role, as the one who is to come, always to the fore. It is God who remains the ultimate end of history (1 Cor 15:28).

THE FIRST VISION (1:9–20)

1:9 I, John, your brother, who share with you the distress, the kingdom, and the endurance we have in Jesus, found myself on the island called Patmos because I proclaimed God's word and gave testimony to Jesus.

1:10 I was caught up in spirit on the Lord's day and heard behind me a voice as loud as a trumpet,

1:11 which said, "Write on a scroll what you see and send it to the seven churches: to Ephesus, Smyrna, Pergamum, Thyatira, Sardis, Philadelphia, and Laodicea."

1:12 Then I turned to see whose voice it was that spoke to me, and when I turned, I saw seven gold lampstands

1:13 and in the midst of the lampstands one like a son of man, wearing an ankle-length robe, with a gold sash around his chest.

1:14 The hair of his head was as white as white wool or as snow, and his eyes were like a fiery flame.

1:15 His feet were like polished brass refined in a furnace, and his voice was like the sound of rushing water.

1:16 In his right hand he held seven stars. A sharp two-edged sword came out of his mouth, and his face shone like the sun at its brightest.

1:17 When I caught sight of him, I fell down at his feet as though dead. He touched me with his right hand and said, "Do not be afraid. I am the first and the last,

1:18 the one who lives. Once I was dead, but now I am alive forever and ever. I hold the keys to death and the netherworld.

1:19 Write down, therefore, what you have seen, and what is happening, and what will happen afterwards.

1:20 This is the secret meaning of the seven stars you saw in my right hand, and of the seven gold lampstands: the seven stars are the angels of the seven churches, and the seven lampstands are the seven churches.

The Vision (vv. 9–20)

I, John, your brother (v. 9): *The seer is a leader in the Christian community who has been banished to the island of Patmos, about seventy miles from coastal Ephesus. His exile was evidently due to the undesirable effects of his preaching and mission. Patmos was a colony to which Rome had frequently sent unsavory voices within its boundaries. The painful lot of the seer is underscored, as he speaks of the distress* (Gr.: thlipsis) *and the long suffering* (Gr.: upomone) *connected with his mission. The terms go beyond mere human discomfort and are connected with the eschatological trial, the final pitched battle between good and evil (Mk 13:3–8; Rev 12:1–6). But he is also a sharer with his readers in "the kingdom," the bright side of the picture, which tells them that final victory is assured because of the already achieved sovereignty of Christ.*

John's mandate is directed to the seven churches (v. 11), all of which are located on the western coast of Asia Minor (Turkey). It is the prophetic spirit that takes hold of the prophet (v.10) and lifts him up to perform a God-directed task, not unlike the prophets before him (Is 42:1; Ez 3:12–15).

The vision of the Christ in glory (vv. 12–16) draws on a number of Old Testament images. Again it is Daniel's son of Man who is central (Dn 7:13), the restored humanity concretized in the risen Jesus. The ankle-length robe is priestly attire (Ex 28:4; 29:5), as is the sash, underscoring Christ's sacerdotal character. His white hair points to his ageless state (Dn 7:9), and his fiery eyes, to the searing and penetrating knowledge of God (Ps 7:10; Jer 17:10; 2:23). The brass-like feet and the tumultuous sound of the voice both derive from Daniel (10:6; Ez 43:2) in describing the heavenly messenger.

The seven lampstands represent the seven churches, and the seven stars in the figure's hand, the angels of the churches. The heavenly figure speaks the Word of God, as the two-edged sword evidences (Heb 4:12). As the heavenly messenger revives the prostrate figure of the seer (v. 17), we are reminded of the extent to which Daniel (10:10) has come into play in this initial vision. In this series of images, Christ is clearly identified as the messenger of the Lord, the one who enunciates the Word, the priestly leader of past, present, and future, the firstborn of the dead. It is he who will now express and interpret the symbols of the book. He is clearly a heavenly figure in majesty and splendor, and yet he walks in the midst of the lampstands, touching the human lives that people the seven churches.

LIVING WITH IMAGES

As the Book of Revelation begins, there are three key players: the seer John, Christ, and God. Each of them has a certain timeless quality. On the very human side, we are all like John, living out our lives with their share of joy and sorrow, under the overarching presence of the invisible and eternal God and his visible and truly human son, Jesus the Lord. Everything in our life is ultimately directed to God "through Jesus Christ our Lord." After all, isn't that the way we pray? And when history draws to a close, it is to God alone that all things will become subject, including Christ himself, as the kingdom is handed over to the Father, with God becoming "all in all" (1 Cor 15:23–28). We can only speak of all this in images; we simply have neither the experience nor the words to express adequately the reality. What we know is that we shall be immersed in the God who has called us into being and for whom we are ultimately destined.

Some of the finest, most upright people we know say that they are dreadfully frightened of death. It is not primarily a fear of judgment; it is because the future is such an unknown. Even with faith, we see now only "through a glass darkly." There is nothing wrong with admitting such a fear. It is a perfectly natural feeling. And it is precisely here that faith enters to engage in the struggle. "Oh Lord, I do believe; help my unbelief." Revelation tells us that the future is mystery, and for all that we do to try and concretize it, mystery it will remain. With all its mind-boggling imagery, Revelation ultimately leaves it with "the Alpha and Omega, the one who is and who was and who is to come." God alone will ultimately bring it all together. In the time of history's greatest triumphs and tragedies, he has always been there. And if process theology has even a modicum of truth, then he also suffers with us. It is hard to believe in a God who was simply a distant onlooker at the Holocaust. And for all the uncertainties that beset us in the present age, God is the one who will be there when it is all over. How we would love to have clearer answers, a real preview of coming attractions. But then where would faith be? The one God has given us only one clear insight into the whole meaning of life and death, and that is Christ, who is our singular "window on God."

And it is because of our faith that we are full of hope. John, the prophetic visionary, was banished to a Roman penal colony for teachings that were anathema to the empire. And we are about to look at the pictures he has painted. Frightening and jarring as they often are, with enough *Sturm und Drang* to keep a surrealist painter enthralled, these images are still the work of a man of great hope, who lived through very difficult times. Without benefit of two millennia of Christian history, at the very dawn of the new era, he is full of hope and dedicated to the proposition that God will ultimately triumph. If we are not also children of hope in a world whose values so often run amuck, whose independence of God and indifference to his reign set humanity on a disastrously downward spiral, then our faith counts for very little. How do we see our faith—simply an adherence to a creed? A form of religious identity? Or is it truly rooted in the belief that Christ is alive and real, the source of a new life and vision, the one who can truly fashion a better world?

And look at the Christ who is depicted in the first chapter. With his hair white as wool, he is ageless; with his feet of brass he is stable and permanent; with his voice like running water, he is refreshing, nourishing, life-giving. Christ is the anchor of our life, the same yesterday, today, and forever (Heb 13:8). He inspired a Paul, a Benedict, a Francis, Teresa (all three, if you will), a Dorothy Day—in Assisi, Avila, Lisieux, Calcutta, and New York. And they speak for countless thousands of other men and women who have lived their faith through the ages. And we should never become so despondent that we fail to trust that other truly Christian spirits lie before us in ages yet to come.

Christ is ageless in the sense that he remains the same "yesterday, today, and forever" (Heb 13:8). What God has accomplished in him remains always; for the atonement of sins there is but one eternal sacrifice. And the basic truth that Jesus has imparted in his life and teaching remains unaltered throughout the ages. But permanence does not mean stagnation. Change is part of any living organism, and the church is no different. As culture and theology interface, new and valuable insights will continue to enrich the Christian message. Biblical studies will continue to explore the multifaceted world of inspired composition to broaden our understanding of scripture's original intent and its meaning for today. Our basic moral principles must address new realities connected with a technological age, looking for answers in a world of human conduct that has become increasingly complex. But we are strengthened in our efforts in realizing that the son of Man with those "feet of polished brass" remains always with us.

What emerges with particular vividness in this opening chapter of Revelation is the emphasis on witness. John has been exiled to Patmos because he "proclaimed God's word and gave testimony to Jesus." *Testimony, witness, martyrdom* are all derived from the same Greek word. Yet John recognizes that Christ himself is the primary "faithful witness," in his fidelity to God's purpose and mission, even though it led him to death. A tragic death only heightens awareness of the importance of the message, as evidenced in the case of Gandhi and Martin Luther King, Jr. And what is the centerpiece of that message of Jesus? It emphasizes the value of the person over the law, a human destiny that is immortal, a forgiveness that knows no bounds, and a love for humankind that is all inclusive. And it was to that message that Christ committed himself unwaveringly. As Paul puts it, Christ was not "Yes" one minute and "No" the next, but rather the unqualified "Yes" to God (cf. 2 Cor 1:19). It is from that commitment of Jesus that John of Patmos derives his strength.

Nothing is clearer than the need for steadfast witness in our times. Good beginnings that soon falter are all too frequently the case today. Other times were characterized by a fidelity to marriage, family, and church, which contributed mightily to making us what we are as a people. And yet today, it seems, it is difficult to stay at the helm when the sea becomes turbulent. It happens in so many areas of life today. Personal satisfaction is paramount; hardship and pain are to be avoided. The tragic results are there for all to see; the whole fabric of society is worn. But Christ remains "the faithful witness." Does this feature of Christian discipleship cut deeply into our faith vision? Do we remember that even etymologically the difference between witness and martyrdom is one of degree not essence? Witness may never carry any of us to martyrdom, but the patient endurance of pain and hardship is unavoidable in any human or spiritual pursuit. Or as one sage has put it, "It's not the final judgment I fear; it's getting there." In our faith engagement we need to keep our eyes riveted on the Christ who remained faithful.

Questions on the Images of Christ

1. What significance do you attach to the various images applied to Christ in the first chapter of Revelation?

2. In what sense do all Christians enjoy a royal and priestly role?

3. How do you understand the second coming of Christ?

4. In the first chapter, what is the meaning of Christ's priestly garb?

5. In what sense are both God and Jesus eternal in Revelation?

6. John of Patmos was an exile for the truth. Can you think of any comparable "exiles" in today's world?

MESSAGES TO SEVEN CHURCHES (2:1–3:22)

Although seven specific churches in Asia Minor are indicated as the destinaries, it is clear that the content of each letter is directed to all the churches (viz. 2:7). A careful reading indicates that the challenges and problems are applicable to the early church as a whole and give a certain inclusiveness to the message. Certain common features are worthy of note before commenting on the individual messages.

   • The cities. *There are seven in all, symbolizing completeness or wholeness. They are about forty miles apart, coastal centers of Roman life (forums, law courts, commerce). Because of the affluence and pagan influence, it was particularly difficult to live Christian values, which clearly conflicted with those of the environs. This conflict is concretized in Revelation with the contrary symbolism of Jerusalem and Babylon representing the basic Christian choice between good and evil.*

   • The angel. *Here the figure is more than a messenger (Dn 10:2–14, 20–21); it is more a protector or guardian of the church addressed. Just as the angel stands for the church, so too the seer is sim-*

ply a mouthpiece of the Lord, a conduit through which the message passes.

• Christ *is the speaker throughout, identified in the symbolic terms that appear repeatedly in the book. He is represented as being wholly conversant with the situation of each church, and the moral mandates presented rest on the salvific action of Christ, who has died and risen on behalf of the churches.*

• The letter itself. *The content is a mixture of praise and blame, promises and threats, with only Smyrna and Philadelphia receiving unqualified praise. There is a certain adaptation of the words of Jesus from the Gospels. The ultimate victory of the cause of righteousness is as evident in the letters as in the book itself.*

THE LIFE SITUATION IN THE CHURCHES

The churches are under persecution in expectation of the last and greatest trial that looms on the horizon. Tribulation (Gr.: thlipsis) *is the order of the day. The image presented is that of a small religious community in the face of pagan cult and culture, divinization of the emperor, and a hostile synagogue. All of this is but a miniature presentation of the larger eschatological battle with Satan and his forces (2:8; 3:9; 2:13).*

There is also a developing split within the community itself in the presence of adherents rallying around certain misinformed "apostles" (not to be identified with the twelve). These wrongsayers and seducers, variously identified as Nicolaitans, Balaam, and Jezebel, seemingly favor "inculturation"–cultural festivals, eating sacrificial meats, acceptance of emperor worship, and a totally realized eschatology. In line with Stoic sentiment, they saw the Christian life as internal, with little reference to external conduct. The community is called to reject such people, to experience an authentic metanoia *in their lives, and to see perseverance and continued endurance* (Gr.: upomone) *as essential to their calling. All of this flows from a triune theology with God (enthroned), Christ (ascendant to the throne), and Christians (called to be attendants at the throne, even if martyrdom be required).*

EPHESUS (2:1–7)

2:1 "To the angel of the church in Ephesus, write this: "'The one who holds the seven stars in his right hand and walks in the midst of the seven gold lampstands says this:

2:2 "I know your works, your labor, and your endurance, and that you cannot tolerate the wicked; you have tested those who call themselves apostles but are not, and discovered that they are impostors.

2:3 Moreover, you have endurance and have suffered for my name, and you have not grown weary.

2:4 Yet I hold this against you: you have lost the love you had at first.

2:5 Realize how far you have fallen. Repent, and do the works you did at first. Otherwise, I will come to you and remove your lampstand from its place, unless you repent.

2:6 But you have this in your favor: you hate the works of the Nicolaitans, which I also hate.

2:7 "'"Whoever has ears ought to hear what the Spirit says to the churches. To the victor I will give the right to eat from the tree of life that is in the garden of God."'"

The Lord Jesus is presented as the omnipotent One, holding the seven stars or angels of the churches in the palm of his hand and yet, as the incarnate God, present to his people as he walks among the lampstands that represent the seven churches (v. 1). The Ephesian Christians, situated in one of Asia Minor's important cities, are commended on a number of scores. Theirs is an active faith characterized by an assiduous expression of conviction (works, labor), as well as endurance in the face of persecution. They have turned away from impostors whose lack of orthodoxy is patent and whose teaching is at odds with the received faith (vv. 2–3), perhaps a reference to the Nicolaitans, a heterodox group in first century Christianity (v. 6). But there is a shadow side as well. They have lost that initial sense of charity that binds all things together (v. 4). We can only surmise what it is that the author has in mind. Have the Ephesians become so taken up with the wrongdoers that they have lost sight of the primacy of love? At any rate, they are called to repentance (Gr.: metanoein), *a reversal of attitude and a move in a new direction. Their perseverance therein is certain to lead to eternal life. This is spoken of in terms of the Genesis* tree of life *(Gn 2:9), which granted immortality to God's favored ones and is here transposed to another key, that is, the eternal life in the Spirit conferred by the risen Christ (v. 7). Failure to do so will lead to the lampstand's being withdrawn, that is, the abolition of their recognition within the Christian community (v. 5).*

CONSTANT BUT...

In many ways what is said of Ephesus could be applied to any one of us today, or to any of our churches. Certainly the church in that city had suffered more than its share with persecution from without and division from within. In spite of it all, they have stayed their course and not abandoned ship. And for this they are justly commended. But now they have dropped anchor, and while buffeted by an occasional wind, they remain largely motionless. This may find expression in hostile attitudes, but the real problem is a listless and passive spirit. They are no longer active players in the drama that is unfolding around them. Therefore, John calls them to a new start, a radical conversion of life.

Though we lack a detailed picture of the situation at Ephesus, the general lines are clear enough and bear a resemblance to our life and culture today. Many of us who grew up in the earlier part of this century remember clearly the effort to maintain Catholic identity in the face of a secular and sometimes hostile culture. Catholicism was the fastest growing religion in the country, but it was not welcome in some quarters. Catholics retrenched and nurtured their own culture. Not only was the church a center of worship, it embraced education, works of charity, and even social life. In a real sense, it formed a culture within a culture. It was clearly a church on the move with its own solid infrastructure. Churches and schools were built, paid for, and utilized—all at the adherents' expense. There was a laity educated in the faith and capable of articulating its basic tenets and enunciating its moral principles. Vocations to the priesthood and religious life abounded.

But then things changed, indeed with a certain inevitability. Catholics identified, to an ever-increasing degree, with the prevailing culture, reaching an apogee in the early 1960s with the election of the first Catholic president. What might be termed "the Catholic ghetto" was gradually disappearing, as American Catholicism became more and more mainstream. There were many positive features connected with this transition. Catholics became more involved in public life, more engaged in the issues that touch all Americans, and were better understood by the broader population. But there were also losses when the struggle for recognition was largely over. We had blended too readily with features of the dominant culture that were negative and even perilous.

Today Catholics are impressive in their numbers. Church attendance, while not the best, is considerably higher than in many other parts of the world. Yet, there is no denying the fact that many of our people today are religiously inarticulate and poorly educated in the principles of the faith. Certainly there is a greater lay involvement in the life of the church: burgeoning ministries, outreach programs, and religious formation. Liturgical reform since the Vatican Council has been widespread and impressive. But on many moral issues, the body of Catholics differs little or nothing from the general population. Many Catholics have withdrawn from active church participation; others participate half-heartedly at best. Like the Ephesians, we get mixed reviews. A history of constancy and fidelity, but also rather worn at the edges. Energy on one side and weariness on the other. While we may still be faithful to the Sunday "obligation," do we not cut corners in the way we live each day?

Like the church in Ephesus, we are called to conversion. This was a central message of Vatican II, and at the dawn of a new millennium the Church issues the call once again. And the great consolation connected with this summons is the adjective that accompanies "conversion." That word is *ongoing*. We never reach the finish line; there is no plateau from which we stop and look out. While it means that the journey is never finished, it also means that we can always pick up and start anew. We may not be able to solve all the church's ills, but there is something we can do about our own lives. To strengthen our life in the Spirit, opportunities abound: concern for a homebound person, teaching a catechism class, joining a hospice or bereavement group, or bringing communion to the sick. It may be a question of strengthening our business ethics, our domestic church which is the home, or our personal relationships. We may need more time to pray. What was true of Ephesus is true of us. We are not all that bad. But we may not take holiness seriously, and holiness is what it is all about.

Reflections on Ephesus

1. Inculturation as a process has its pros and cons. Discuss some of these.

2. Conversion can be understood in a number of ways. What is the biblical understanding?

3. How can we succeed in dealing with opposition and differences in charity?

4. What are some of our modern "tribulations"?

5. Explain how in your daily life there is room for constant and patient endurance.

6. How could it be said today: "You have lost the love you had at first"?

SMYRNA (2:8–11)

2:8 "To the angel of the church in Smyrna, write this: " 'The first and the last, who once died but came to life, says this:

2:9 "I know your tribulation and poverty, but you are rich. I know the slander of those who claim to be Jews and are not, but rather are members of the assembly of Satan.

2:10 Do not be afraid of anything that you are going to suffer. Indeed, the devil will throw some of you into prison, that you may be tested, and you will face an ordeal for ten days. Remain faithful until death, and I will give you the crown of life.

2:11 ' "Whoever has ears ought to hear what the Spirit says to the churches. The victor shall not be harmed by the second death." ' "

Smyrna (present day Izmir), about thirty miles north of Ephesus, is a beautiful coastal city. It had a long pre-Christian history and was destroyed and rebuilt by Alexander the Great. It was strongly allied with Rome and had a large Jewish community.

The speaker, the risen Christ, speaks of his timeless presence and his salvific death (v. 8; 1:17f). Persecution dogs the Christians at Smyrna; they are poor but paradoxically rich by reason of their faith (v. 9; Jas 2:5; 2 Cor 8:9). The Jewish community in the city had a reputation for cruelty and played a part in the martyrdom of Polycarp (ca. 155). They are not here accorded the title of authentic Jews but are said to be of the "assembly of Satan" (v. 9; Jn 8:44). Persecution will be severe, even though short-lived ("ten days," cf. Dn 1:12), secondary causes of which are bypassed as Satan himself is presented as the agent (v. 10). But fidelity will lead to eternal life, where there will be no need to fear the "second death" or eternal condemnation (Lk 12:4f). There are no reproaches in the letter to Smyrna.

FAITHFUL UNTO DEATH

The beautiful coastal city of Izmir in modern Turkey was the Smyrna of early Christianity, linked with the name of Polycarp, and, of course, Ephesus, thirty miles to the south. As we have seen, there are only words of praise and support for Smyrna in John's letter. Persecution was the reality most in evidence, the small Christian community evidently beset by a strong Jewish sectarianism. Imprisonment, torture, even death hover on the horizon; the most the author can do is to encourage trust, based on the strong conviction that this is not the end.

Hatred and killing have become so much a part of the history of humanity that we are almost anesthetized to the brutal reality. The number of lives taken in war during the last century alone is staggering, almost incredible. In a visit to the Circus Maximus in Rome we hear recounted the story of countless Christians who were crucified to assuage Roman hatred. And yet the numbers are infinitesimally small in comparison to the millions of innocent men, women, and children who died useless and cruel deaths in the twentieth century simply because they were the innocent victims of conflict. The Jewish population certainly suffered immense losses, but many others died as well, people who could never be considered combatants. The country of Poland alone, caught between Nazism and Communism, lost hundreds of thousands of people at the hand of hardened invaders. Young military men on all sides died on beachheads, on freezing battlefields, in concentration camps. Under "Catholic" dictators in Latin America, political dissidents in large numbers were not simply arrested and detained; they were never heard from again. And today terrorists take innocent lives to make a political point.

In Revelation we get only the first glimmer of the incredible inhumanity yet to come. Indeed, it may well be asked: How many times have we not witnessed the promised Armageddon? Has not the "end time" appeared in different forms in our own lifetime? Modern technology has brought war into our living rooms and left us unmoved by its dreadful impact. Until war as a human solution to any problem is eliminated, humanity cannot forget the extent to which it is capable of the worst. Human consciousness combined with dreaded scientific possibilities may be moving us slowly toward a human consensus to outlaw warfare. If so, it will ultimately be based on the dignity of every human person.

And so we see war as the solution to nothing. The letter to Ephesus presents the whole issue in microcosm. Do we believe that people have the right to follow their own conscience in peace and tranquility? In this regard the history of Christianity has not always been bright. At Ephesus, Christians suffered at the hands of Jews, but how often have Jews suffered at the hands of Christians? For centuries the church could not uphold religious liberty, because, it was said, "error has no rights." It was Vatican II's statement on religious liberty that placed people and not issues at the center of the picture. Unless the common good is imperiled, people have the right to follow their own conscience and to remain undisturbed. Even those biblical narratives that speak of *herem* or total war, which meant the elimination of all opponents, military or otherwise, in Israelite warfare, are difficult for us to read today. Even though seen as the mindset of the people of the time, and not a God-directed endeavor, we can only regret that divine enlightenment did not penetrate at an earlier date.

Pope Paul VI stood before the United Nations General Assembly and cried out: "War! War! Never again war!" The human voice must be raised to prevent human slaughter at all cost. And this involves all of the life issues: abortion, assisted suicide, capital punishment, as well as war itself. And the reason remains simple: Life is a precious gift and is to be cherished. It underlies the message to Smyrna and resonates throughout the world, increasingly so in these our times.

Reflecting on Death and Life Beyond Smyrna

1. The twentieth century has seen untold death and destruction. How does that fit into your faith vision?

2. Many people ask where God was during the Holocaust. What is your response?

3. Explain how we became rich through Christ's becoming poor.

4. Can we truly incorporate suffering into our moral vision of life?

5. Reflect on the importance of personal fidelity in a very unstable age.

6. How has the nuclear age changed our thinking on war?

PERGAMUM (2:12–17)

2:12 "To the angel of the church in Pergamum, write this: " 'The one with the sharp two-edged sword says this:

2:13 "I know that you live where Satan's throne is, and yet you hold fast to my name and have not denied your faith in me, not even in the days of Antipas, my faithful witness, who was martyred among you, where Satan lives.

2:14 Yet I have a few things against you. You have some people there who hold to the teaching of Balaam, who instructed Balak to put a stumbling block before the Israelites: to eat food sacrificed to idols and to play the harlot.

2:15 Likewise, you also have some people who hold to the teaching of [the] Nicolaitans.

2:16 Therefore, repent. Otherwise, I will come to you quickly and wage war against them with the sword of my mouth.

2:17 " ' "Whoever has ears ought to hear what the Spirit says to the churches. To the victor I shall give some of the hidden manna; I shall also give a white amulet upon which is inscribed a new name, which no one knows except the one who receives it." ' "

A city about forty miles north of Smyrna, Pergamum was a Roman administrative center. Therefore the cult of the emperor played an important part in the religio-cultural life of the citizenry. The speaker is the one who holds the double-edged sword, an instrument of destruction and punishment. It is a metaphor for Yahweh's decree of retribution (vv. 12, 16). Satan's throne *(v. 13): a center of the imperial cult.* My name *(v. 13): Lord, the divine appellative conferred upon Christ with his resurrection-exaltation (Phil 2:9–11). The Christians of Pergamum, in the face of grave persecution, even leading to the martyrdom of a certain Antipas, have never wavered in their commitment to the lordship of Jesus by rendering the same title to the emperor.*

However, with the internal life of the community, they have not done as well. Compromise and syncretism are in the air. They are being tempted by those who claim that eating food offered to idols is licit; Paul himself acknowledged the legality of eating food presented to "no gods" (1 Cor 8:8f), yet he would willingly abstain if his conduct were to give scandal (a stumbling block) (Gr.: skandalon) *to others. This is precisely what is happening in Pergamum (v. 14).* To play the harlot *(v. 14): The reference here is to religious syncretism, that is, abandoning the true God to reverence false gods. The biblical reference is to the sin of Peor (Nm 25:1–3), where false gods and cultic sexual immorality captured the Israelites during their desert journey, for which Balaam is presented as being the instigator in presenting the "stumbling block" to the people (Nm 31:16). Balaam's culpability does not appear in the original account, but his alleged blame is carried into the New Testament at various points (Jude 11; 2 Pt 2:15). However, it is the "stumbling block" that links Balaam with the Pergamum community. The Nicolaitans appear again (v. 15); whether or not they are the proponents of the aforementioned aberrancies is not clear. They are seen, however, as leading the just astray.* Metanoia *is called for, and immediately.*

The reference to the inscribed white stone and the manna (v. 17) has eschatological significance. The stone is inscribed with the Lord's name (3:12) and points to Christian rebirth. The manna reflects the post-exilic Jewish belief that the lost ark of the covenant, the tablets of the law, and the manna, carried away from the temple, were temporarily concealed but would reappear in the final days (cf. Ex 16:31–34; Heb 9:4).

COMPROMISE AND SCANDAL

Another coastal city, present day Bergama, lies north of Izmir and had a considerable importance in Roman times. The picture presented in Revelation is rather mixed; basic fidelity in the midst of a threatening situation, but also a measure of compromise and scandal. As Paul himself indicated, there is nothing wrong with eating meat offered to idols, although conscience might advise otherwise where there is a danger of scandal. Compromise and scandal. About the former we hear much today; about the latter, very little.

Compromise is not a negative quality in itself. In fact, it can be a plus in many instances. It is probably safe to say that in an earlier era of American Catholicism there was very little compromise in matters religious. Religion took preeminence over almost every other factor in life. In larger cities Catholics identified themselves with their parish (St. Monica, St. George) rather than with their neighborhood. One might have Protestant or Jewish friends, but would never attend their services, be part of their wedding party, or—perish the thought—sing in their choir or play the organ in their church. Gradually this changed, with the increased emphasis on what unites rather than divides us. Ecumenism became a household word, and relations between faiths are now greatly improved. And this touches on but one aspect of life.

A certain measure of compromise is wholesome and unquestionably positive. On the other hand, distinctiveness is an important quality as well, and there are areas around which there can be no compromise. Determining exactly at what point this takes place is a walk through a minefield, with a paucity of ready answers. It is never easy to decide at what point we cannot move from the center in determining those areas where adaptation or inculturation is suitable. Intransigence around every point or the failure to distinguish adequately between doctrine and discipline simply leads to a permanent standoff. Yet, an emphasis on compromise that leads to the dilution of principle is unthinking and ultimately disastrous. Distinctiveness is the very nature of Christianity. The holiness or otherness of God becomes tangible in the life of a people whose beliefs, ethics, and worship set them apart. Compromise that simply "goes with the flow" is alien to a faith that points beyond. And yet in doctrine, morality, and worship there always has been and will continue to be development. Every doctrine is a human insight into God, valid in itself but never exhaustive of the underlying Reality. Moral principles today interface with incredibly complex developments in the technical and behavioral sciences, which are bound to lead to new ways of applying the principles. Worship honors a transcendent God in the language and customs of many different peoples, and there too adaptation is unavoidable.

It might be said that change within the church is not really a compromise. But in a way it is, in as much as it departs from a standard position in the interests of responding to new values and insights that emerge. And in the minds of not a few people within the church, it is a compromise that is unwarranted and unwelcome. How else explain the vigorous, even strident reaction that is so often given prominence today? A fixed essentialist mindset sees all features of church life as having a certain immutability. This means that change is suspect; adaptation becomes equated with betrayal. It is compromise at its worst. What is utterly simplistic about such reaction is its lack of an historical sense, the realization that the church has changed in countless ways throughout the centuries. Indeed, change is the true sign of life. Are there limits to change and compromise? Certainly. And this is why the task of those involved in the theological disciplines is so delicate. They must realize that new expressions of belief and the incorporation of new insights are an essential part of their task, but it is a pursuit that is ever conscious of a sacred patrimony.

This, of course, calls for responsibility in striving for a sense of continuity and organic development.

But there was also *scandal* at Pergamum, a word that does not enjoy common coinage today. We are said to be living in an age that is beyond scandal. But we lose sight of it only to our own disadvantage. Scandal sets forth an aberrant form of behavior in such wise that another is made to "stumble" or is deflected from doing good. Its seriousness is set forth clearly enough in the scriptures themselves, and experience itself bears it out. Attitudes weaken; principles bend and are relativized; sinful proclivities hold sway. It is one thing to concede to weakness in one's own life; it is quite another to lead others on a path of unrighteousness. And it is important to remember that scandal is also given through an attitude of indifference. When those who are charged with responsibility fail to shoulder it, as when heads of families fail to give the due religious formation to their children, then the efforts of others to foster moral principles ring hollow indeed.

One hears so little about scandal today because the presumption exists that people, even the young, are somehow beyond it. But it is a claim that needs to be questioned. Pastoral experience bears out the fact that people today, especially youth, are highly impressionable. One can be led astray or be led to a life of virtue. Society clamors for positive role models, those who not only lay claim to moral principle but give it expression in their daily life. We are still a very impressionable people, for well or ill. Just as the angel was reproached about the "stumbling blocks" present in Pergamum and received a summons to repentance, we are all given pause to reflect on our lives as individuals and as a community. The question is raised: To what extent is my own *mea culpa* in order?

Thinking about Fidelity and Compromise

1. Compromise can be seen in a positive or negative light. How would you explain these two aspects?

2. Christ is the "faithful witness." Can you think of anyone in modern times who might be similarly identified?

3. Review the story of Balaam in the Book of Numbers in the light of its use in Revelation.

4. Cite ways in which you feel that scandal may be given in our day.

5. We all need positive role models. Can you cite one who stands out in your own life?

THYATIRA (2:18–29)

2:18 "To the angel of the church in Thyatira, write this: " 'The Son of God, whose eyes are like a fiery flame and whose feet are like polished brass, says this:

2:19 "I know your works, your love, faith, service, and endurance, and that your last works are greater than the first.

2:20 Yet I hold this against you, that you tolerate the woman Jezebel, who calls herself a prophetess, who teaches and misleads my servants to play the harlot and to eat food sacrificed to idols.

2:21 I have given her time to repent, but she refuses to repent of her harlotry.

2:22 So I will cast her on a sickbed and plunge those who commit adultery with her into intense suffering unless they repent of her works.

2:23 I will also put her children to death. Thus shall all the churches come to know that I am the searcher of hearts and minds and that I will give each of you what your works deserve.

2:24 But I say to the rest of you in Thyatira, who do not uphold this teaching and know nothing of the so-called deep secrets of Satan: on you I will place no further burden,

2:25 except that you must hold fast to what you have until I come.

2:26 " ' "To the victor, who keeps to my ways until the end,
I will give authority over the nations.

2:27 He will rule them with an iron rod.
Like clay vessels will they be smashed,

2:28 Just as I received authority from my Father. And to him I will give the morning star.

2:29 " ' "Whoever has ears ought to hear what the Spirit says to the churches." ' "

Thyatira was an industrial city famous for its fabrics and dyes (Acts 16:14), as well as its guilds. It was located some forty miles southeast of Pergamum. Our lack of information on the founding of the church there means we have little background to the problems here addressed.

Here Christ is referred to in familiar New Testament language. In what is a clear Christological affirmation, he is simply identified as the Son of God (v. 18). Once again his penetrating omniscience is underscored (fiery eyes), as well as his permanence and stability (brass feet). (Cf. 1:14–15). Christianity was not an idle pursuit in Thyatira, a city cited for its good works (Gr.: erga), its love (Gr.: agapen), its faith (Gr.: pistin), service (Gr.: diakonian), and endurance (Gr.: upomonen) (v. 19). This is a litany of virtues repeatedly extolled in the New Testament writings. Good works are an expression of faith (Jas 2:16–18); in the context, charity looks to love of neighbor (1 Cor 13). Faith is an authentic belief that is upheld in the midst of a foreign and nonbelieving culture. Service stands at the heart of the Christian life (Rom 15:25, 31; 1 Cor 16:15; Acts 6:1–7); it is a ministry that looks to both the table and the Word in the interest of the upbuilding of the community. Endurance appears repeatedly in Revelation and looks to hold fast in the midst of persecution.

Yet, despite the good report, difficulties have arisen in the area of improper compromise. It is here that the image of Jezebel comes into play (vv. 20–23). The wife of King Ahab, Jezebel flagrantly disregarded true Yahwism by leading Israel into idolatry through the worship of Baal, which was looked upon as religious adultery (2 Kgs 9:22). This explains the metaphorical use of adultery here. The same is true of the Jezebel image itself. Rather than a reference to a specific individual, it is best understood as a generic reference to those, like the Nicolaitans, who are leading the early Christians on a path of religious infidelity. In the absence of repentance, they and their adherents will suffer the final lot of definitive punishment and separation (vv. 21–23). Those who ally themselves with the Spirit in discerning "the deep things of God" (1 Cor 2:10), and not following religious syncretism in plummeting the "deep secrets of Satan" (v. 24) (in words that have Gnostic overtones) will have no further burdens, but will be accorded the victory. In language taken from the royal psalter, the faithful one will be accorded "authority over the nations," with the insignia of royal power and force (vv. 26–27; Ps 2:8–9). All of this is authority that Christ himself has received from the Father (v. 28) and that is in turn conferred on the triumphant believer. The morning star *(v. 28): A probable reference to final resurrection, of which Jesus himself is the prototype (cf. 22:16).*

A SPECTRUM OF VIRTUES

Despite the seductions of Jezebel, there is much to commend the Christian community of Thyatira. They are rich in the virtues that repeatedly come to the fore in the New Testament accounts of the early church. Faith and love are immediately cited, pointing to a community that is rooted in God-directedness, a deep centered belief that God has acted definitively in Christ Jesus, whose death, resurrection, and expected return are central to its very existence. Yet faith without concomitant works is a very empty faith, something which has not been the case in Thyatira. Service and endurance come to the fore as pivotal expressions of faith. *Diakonia* or service is intimately linked with the giftedness of God toward all of creation, but preeminently present in the gift of his Son. Loving service toward one another is but an extension of what makes the mystery of God what it is. This is seen as the attitude or posture of Jesus himself in generous self-giving toward all, in his being the "foot washer" at the Johannine final supper. *Upomone* or endurance is a value situated in a climate of persecution and rejection, to which the early Christians were subjected from Jews and Romans. It says much more than passive acceptance of a bad situation; it looks to an ardent adherence to Christ with a faith that makes all things sufferable and embraces the believer in a spirit of equanimity and inner serenity.

IN A MODERN KEY

These positive qualities present in the Thyatirans, a minority community, in the midst of a fair amount of hostility, can give us pause today. Roman Catholicism in the United States is the largest single religious denomination. In view of its numbers, one would expect its impact to be stronger than is actually the case. There are always dangers inherent in becoming the dominant force; the history of Western Christianity has shown that clearly enough. The early Christians, even though small in number, were significant for their spirit of service and love of one another. Catholicism today is admired in many quarters because it has a certain firmness and stability, a set of beliefs that clearly identify it. There is a clarity of vision that elicits respect. But by being in a majority position and emerging decisively from the Catholic "ghetto," we have become respectable as well and in many ways have blended with the contemporary culture in ways that are anything but helpful. In the small communities of Revelation, Christians were frequently the "salt of the earth" and the "light of the world." One wonders if those are the images that emerge today. Regrettably we are guilty of a great deal of Sunday morning Catholicism, with secular pursuits and values dominating our lives the remaining days of the week.

Sacrifice is not a popular word today. But this is precisely what *diakonia* means: called to be at the service of our sisters and brothers as was Christ himself. From this charge no one is exempt. Without doubt, our parishes and dioceses are involved in outreach in many different forms. But what percentage of our people sees this as something that touches them? When we compare our organization lists with the numbers for Mass attendance, we are faced with the fact that we fall far short of the mark. To recognize service as one of the essential marks of Christianity means that each of us must be alert to human need and our own ability to respond. Our most affluent societies have depressing pockets of poverty and need, in one form or another, that call us to Christian consciousness. Once we take stock of our resources in the face of authentic need, then we can be moved to link mind and heart; faith and action will quickly be bound together. We must bring ourselves to understand that Christianity is more than avoiding sin; it is above all a religion of doing good. And this is not something that springs from political awareness. Government may remind us but it does not offer the basic incentive. Outreach is as old as the scriptures themselves, and is deeply woven into the teaching of the New Testament. The Thyatirans, for all their difficulties, had grasped the message.

It would be wrong to understand biblical endurance in a passive sense. It is not simply "putting up" with something. Conversely, it does mean "being in there for the long haul" because of God's trustworthiness. It does not mean relishing the distasteful nor does it mean running from it. Once again it makes sense only in the light of Christ. The God who draws near us is a God who knows what suffering means, and it is from that point that we draw the courage to endure with equanimity. I am reminded of a woman whom I knew in Milan. She had been bedridden with an incurable paralysis for more than twenty years and was incapable of doing anything for herself. What never failed to impress me was the incredible cheerfulness with which she always received her visitors. Or I think of the seminarian whom I taught. The young man was crippled for life by a football accident, paralyzed from the neck down. His indomitable spirit lifted the heart of the entire seminary community. Or the married woman whose life of grinding poverty and the absence of basic human comforts offered little solace, yet her sense of commitment was unwavering. Experience offers us all many examples. And let this be our prayer: When that moment of trial comes in our own life, as come it must, may we see it in Pauline terms as a "fellowship in his sufferings" (Phil 3:10). The last word will be God's. "To the victor who keeps to my ways until the end, I will give authority over the nations. To him I will give the 'morning star.'"

Being Faithful at Thyatira

1. What do works, faith, love, service, and endurance mean for the Christian today?

2. Who is "Jezebel" in today's world? In our culture?

3. What implications does Jesus' act of footwashing have for your own life? For your understanding of God?

4. Can you describe the relationship between faith and action?

5. What examples of faithful endurance have you known?

SARDIS (3:1-6)

3:1 "To the angel of the church in Sardis, write this: "'The one who has the seven spirits of God and the seven stars says this: "I know your works, that you have the reputation of being alive, but you are dead.

3:2 Be watchful and strengthen what is left, which is going to die, for I have not found your works complete in the sight of my God.

3:3 Remember then how you accepted and heard; keep it, and repent. If you are not watchful, I will come like a thief, and you will never know at what hour I will come upon you.

3:4 However, you have a few people in Sardis who have not soiled their garments; they will walk with me dressed in white, because they are worthy.

3:5 "'"The victor will thus be dressed in white, and I will never erase his name from the book of life but will acknowledge his name in the presence of my Father and of his angels.

3:6 "'"Whoever has ears ought to hear what the Spirit says to the churches."'"

Here the picture is quite different. We see what happens when endurance is not at work. Sardis was about twenty miles southeast of Thyatira, a one-time capital of Lydia. Taken by Cyrus (546 B.C.), it became a center of Persian life. It was prosperous, luxurious, and licentious.

Here Christ holds the seven stars (3:1) and controls as well the seven spirits (5:6), all of which points to him as the life-giver. The addressees: Sardis has only the appearance of life; it is actually dead, without a living faith. Its "works" are present (v. 2), but they are empty and not expressive of a faith in action. They must revert to their beginnings, their original "hearing" and "acceptance"; they will recapture their earlier spirit only by repenting. With the images of the unexpected frequent in the New Testament (thief, night, hour; Mt 24:42ff; Mk

13:33), the people are reminded that lack of repentance can lead to sudden death.

But here as elsewhere there is the salvation of the remnant, the elect of God (vv. 4–5). They are clothed in white, the symbol of baptismal innocence and victory (Dn 7:9; Mk 9:3); Christians have "put on" the Lord Jesus, clothing being closely identified with the wearer (Col 3:12ff). The name is inscribed in the "book of life," which in Old Testament thought looked to an extension of temporal life (Ex 32:32f; Ps 69:28; Is 4:3). Here the names are those of the redeemed, the saved (13:8; 17:8; 20:12, 15).

"YOU SEEM TO BE ALIVE"

The situation in Sardis is as familiar as it is lamentable; the reputation is positive but the reality, negative. The community seems to be alive but it is dead. Through the seer God makes an appeal for the little good that remains to be strengthened. There is something about all of this that sounds strangely familiar; indeed, many of our own lives have been touched by the same ailment. Milestones in our life keep us intensely focused, and difficulties often arise when the milestones are no longer there. On a personal note, I still remember vividly my advancement toward final profession and priesthood. Every year along the way, there was another step, celebrated liturgically, that brought me closer to my goal. Finally that glorious day of ordination dawned, on which everything conspired to make it the day of days. This was followed by academic accomplishments and other important moments that made life a great adventure and kept moral consciousness at a high level. But then the major events were no more; life adopted a normal, and often "humdrum" pace. Repetition, routine, sameness—these became the order of the day. Year follows year, and the clock of life ticks on as the aging process continues. This is a very critical moment in life, from a human as well as spiritual perspective. It may be termed midlife ennui. Here directions in life often take subtle turns. Weariness can lead to compromise, a settling for the less than best, a gradual decline in "doing the good." Outwardly everything looks fine—efficiency, good order, professionalism—but within something has gone awry. The excitement has gone. Before God, we know that we are not where we should be. We are citizens of Sardis. "You have the reputation of being alive but you are dead."

To live a double life is to induce a spiritual schizophrenia. But it is not all that rare. First, conscience has gone to sleep, if it has not already vanished. After all, if one is going to live hypocritically, there is no sense in being tortured by it. And so sweet logic is applied. Just weigh the reasoning: "Things are not that bad. There are reasons why I act this way, and there are countless others who do the same." "I am not the first man in history to betray his wife." "I have certain needs and God understands that." "The money that I take is hardly worth mentioning when one considers the assets of my company." "Expense accounts are meant to be padded."

THE POSSIBILITY OF CONVERSION

Life can continue on a rather normal keel, but internally "rigor mortis" has set in. The facade stays up; the mask is in place; but it is all a shell. It is at this point that the central virtue of the New Testament, so important in Revelation, comes to the fore. *Metanoia* can come into play for the asking. This is the lesson of the *felix culpa* or the happy fault. Sin, as serious or habitual as it may be, can become a saving grace. Regardless of where we are on the spectrum of alienation, God is there for us. It is the good shepherd who never fails to extend a "welcome home." There is great honesty in being able to face our weaknesses. We can truly become better people if we look sin in the face and name it. In a true and sincere turning of our life over to God, realizing that we are helpless of ourselves, we can begin anew the journey of holiness. The prodigal son did not begin the journey home to his father with perfect contrition. Indeed, there is no indication that he had any sorrow. But he was tenderly welcomed. To turn to God in love is itself a great sign of virtue. I once asked a priest who had spent many years of his life reconciling people to God in confession what he had learned from the experience. He answered unhesitatingly, "I have learned much about the goodness of people."

With conversion we break free of hypocrisy. In the latter case, when all seems well and it is not, the burning question remains: Is faith present? After all, humans may look in the face, but God looks at the heart (1 Sm 16:7). And how often the hidden truth of an alienated life somehow overtakes us anyway, sometimes with devastating effects. For countless reasons, it is better to face our weakness honestly, turn our lives over to God, and let the healing process begin. It is salutary and even humanly healthy. In our relativizing moral climate today, it is important to keep our faith values before our eyes. It was needed at Sardis, as it is needed in our time. Yes, we need it as a society, but we may very well need it as individuals. The burning question is there: Am I truly honest with God?

Further Reflections on Fidelity

1. In what way is prosperity a danger?

2. How is "the midlife crisis" an opportunity for growth?

3. Why is repentance more important than good works?

4. Is compromise good or bad? What about compromising your ideals?

5. What does it mean to "put on" the Lord Jesus? How would you apply this to your life?

PHILADELPHIA (3:7–13)

3:7 "To the angel of the church in Philadelphia, write this:
"'The holy one, the true,
who holds the key of David,
who opens and no one shall close,
who closes and no one shall open,
says this:

3:8 "'"I know your works (behold, I have left an open door before you, which no one can close). You have limited strength, and yet you have kept my word and have not denied my name.

3:9 Behold, I will make those of the assembly of Satan who claim to be Jews and are not, but are lying, behold I will make them come and fall prostrate at your feet, and they will realize that I love you.

3:10 Because you have kept my message of endurance, I will keep you safe in the time of trial that is going to come to the whole world to test the inhabitants of the earth.

3:11 I am coming quickly. Hold fast to what you have, so that no one may take your crown.

3:12 " ' "The victor I will make into a pillar in the temple of my God, and he will never leave it again. On him I will inscribe the name of my God and the name of the city of my God, the new Jerusalem, which comes down out of heaven from my God, as well as my new name.

3:13 " ' "Whoever has ears ought to hear what the Spirit says to the churches." ' "

Only words of encouragement are given to the Christians of this city, located some thirty miles southeast of Sardis. Founded by Attalus II in the mid-second century before Christ, it was a center of Greek culture. Destroyed by an earthquake in A.D. 17, it was later rebuilt by Tiberias and renamed Neo-Caesarea (modern Alasehir). The speaker, again Christ, is given titles of transcendence (v. 7): "the holy one" (Is 40:25; Rev 4:8), "the true one" (Gr.: alethinos). This points to Christ's faithful, committed, authentic stance (Jn 14:6), also applied to Yahweh himself (Is 65:16). Key of David *(v. 7): Grants entrance to and excludes one from the Messianic banquet, pointing to the plenary authority of the risen Christ.*

The "open door" is immediately granted to the Philadelphia community, that is, access to salvation (v. 8). This group of Christians has been under siege from the local Jews ("assembly of Satan"). Their perseverance will be rewarded with final deliverance, at which time their opponents will be vanquished while being made aware of Christ's love for his people. There is something simple and singular about the straightforward: "I love you" (v. 9).

Christ has given a "message of endurance," not only in his teaching, but more important, in his life. The Philadelphians have kept to this message, and in the final trial, which is part of the end-time tribulation to which the entire world will be subject, they will reap the much desired deliverance (vv. 10–11; Mt 6:13).

Metaphor is prominent as final salvation of the elect is described. There will be no temple or pillars in the heavenly Jerusalem (21:22), but the victor is designated a "pillar," that is, a person of exalted position in the saved community (Gal 2:9). He will also receive a threefold name inscription: the name, in biblical terms, identifies the person and fixes his or her destiny. The three names signify that the elect belongs to Yahweh, is a citizen of the heavenly Jerusalem, and recognizes Jesus as Lord (v. 12; Phil 2:9–11).

PEOPLE OF LIMITED STRENGTH

There is only encouragement for the Christians of Philadelphia; yet there is nothing about the community that is particularly illustrious. They have "limited strength," and yet have remained faithful. In our daily lives most of the people we know are probably of "limited strength"; they do not perform outstanding deeds, and yet they are always there. They can always be relied upon; in fact, we often feel that undue advantage is taken of them. Their strength may be limited for a variety of reasons. It may well be that illness has taken its toll on their physical resources. They may have had minimal education or lack strong intellectual endowment. People may be undistinguished for any number of reasons, but it all fades into insignificance in the light of their unwavering constancy.

Isn't this the basic stuff of sanctity? Some of us remember the exploits of the saints who were held up for our admiration (and hopeful imitation) in the old Roman breviary. Role models they were in many instances, but they were still light-years away from our plodding efforts. It was impossible to believe that we could ever attain those heights of sanctity. But as years went by we better realized what it means to say that all Christians are called to sanctity, and that it is quite possible to be about very ordinary things and be recorded in "the book of life." Certainly the "little way" of Saint Thérèse of Lisieux gave more immediate access to sanctity to countless people than had previously been thought possible.

The Philadelphians had limited strength and yet showed great endurance. It is not easy to stay on track for the long haul, especially when there is little notice and less affirmation along the way. And yet how many people do we know who do precisely that? And often it is not until they are gone that we realize the immense impact they have made on our lives. Their strength is remarkable, with God clearly at the center of their lives. And that is all that matters. Therein lies the call to holiness for all, regardless of our limited strength. Holiness means realizing how much we are loved and that we have immense value in God's sight. It means reading the story of redemption in the light of our own personal history. The consequent expression of our gratitude is the stuff of sanctity. Our strength may be limited, but our love is vast.

THE PILLAR'S INSCRIPTION

To Philadelphia it was said that the victor would become a pillar in the end-time temple. A pillar stands for stability and strength, and is a logical consequence to endurance. And that end-time pillar is inscribed with the names of God, Jerusalem, and Christ (3:12). These names are a good summary of all that Christianity stands for. The Christians' values are shaped by the fact that God stands behind everything they are. They know when they do well or poorly because God, not the shifting sands of the moment, is their measuring stick. In addition, God has spoken in Christ, the one who inspires and gives the victory. The very expression *cross-bearing* conjures up the image of the one, like us in everything but sin, who has carried his cross before us. As our window on God, Jesus brings God so close that we are never left with the awful nothingness of the agnostic. We do know, and it is because we know that we act. And finally, the inscription Jerusalem for us means "church." It is the church that brings it all to life—the scriptures, the teachings, the sacraments, the community of love. Because it has its human component, the church can make us glad or sad, overjoyed or angry. We certainly do not like everything that happens in this community of believers, which still lives on this side of the Rubicon. But she is a mother, who in her best moments cannot be surpassed. She is with us at our baptism and accompanies us to the grave. And following the "little way" to holiness is only possible because she has given us the map.

God, Christ, and Jerusalem. That sums it all up; everything else is secondary. If there is anything that stands out in "the Philadelphia story," it is that single verity. And it has changed little in two millennia. We have only to look around: we are rubbing shoulders with holiness every day of our lives in those generous people who bring to us salt and light. For reasons probably unmerited, America's Philadelphia has always stood a bit in the shadow of neighboring metropolises. Entertainers didn't like to play there because audiences "sat on their hands." A punster once commented that "Philadelphia is just a yawn on the train between New York and Washington." But the earlier Philadelphia might well say to the latter: "That's quite all right. Status doesn't matter at all. It's not really what counts in life. Remain true to your conviction and stand tall before God, even with your limited strength." The tall and the mighty may one day fall. But like the mighty palm, the just person, rooted in the Lord, will live forever.

Lessons from the Philadelphia Story

1. The New Testament version of the Lord's Prayer reads: "Do not bring us to the trial." What meaning has that for you?

2. Do we know people of "limited strength" who nonetheless struggle mightily?

3. Reflect on the major triangle: God, Christ, and church.

4. Discuss the biblical significance of the name and our own approach to naming children today.

5. The Book of Revelation uses derogatory terms like "the assembly of Satan" for the Jews in Smyrna. How do we understand expressions like this in our time of more positive relations between Christians and Jews?

6. What do we mean by "holiness" as "otherness"?

LAODICEA (3:14–22)

3:14 "To the angel of the church in Laodicea, write this: "'The Amen, the faithful and true witness, the source of God's creation, says this:

3:15 "I know your works; I know that you are neither cold nor hot. I wish you were either cold or hot.

3:16 So, because you are lukewarm, neither hot nor cold, I will spit you out of my mouth.

3:17 For you say, 'I am rich and affluent and have no need of anything,' and yet do not realize that you are wretched, pitiable, poor, blind, and naked.

3:18 I advise you to buy from me gold refined by fire so that you may be rich, and white garments to put on so that your shameful nakedness may not be exposed, and buy ointment to smear on your eyes so that you may see.

3:19 Those whom I love, I reprove and chastise. Be earnest, therefore, and repent.

3:20 "'"Behold, I stand at the door and knock. If anyone hears my voice and opens the door, [then] I will enter his house and dine with him, and he with me.

3:21 I will give the victor the right to sit with me on my throne, as I myself first won the victory and sit with my Father on his throne.

3:22 "'"Whoever has ears ought to hear what the Spirit says to the churches."'"

Laodicea was some forty miles southeast of Philadelphia and was a center of commercial activity: banking, merchandising, and the study of medicine. It was destroyed by an earthquake in A.D. 60 and rose again from its ruins.

The speaker: *Jesus is the* Amen, *the faithful and true witness, with the text itself explaining the meaning of the designation (v. 14; 3:7; Is 65:16). Christ remained totally committed to his mission from the Father and did not waver (cf. 2 Cor 1:17–20).* Source of creation *(v. 14): Literally "the beginning of creation" (Gr.: arche). This points to the pre-existent Christ present with God at the very beginning of the universe (Col 1:15–20).*

The fidelity and commitment of Christ contrast sharply with that of the Laodiceans, who are tepid and half-hearted (vv. 15f), much like the hot spring water from nearby Hierapolis, which was lukewarm by the time it reached Laodicea. The radical demands of the gospel require a clear "Yes" or "No," but from the Laodiceans there comes only a vacillating indecision. This is an attitude which the Lord can only reject ("vomit out of my mouth").

A second problem is affluence (vv. 17ff). Although they parade their rich stature, the irony is that before God, the Laodiceans are poor and wretched. In the familiar language of merchandising, they should do their shopping elsewhere; they should buy from Christ (v. 18).

• True gold: *This is faith (1 Pt 1:7). When tested by fire through hardship, their endurance prevails.*

• White garments: *The symbol of purity and holiness of life, and the clothing of the final victory (3:5; 2 Cor 5:4).*

• Eye ointment: *Laodicea was a center of eye treatment. Here Christ speaks of the vision that comes from the light of faith (Jn 8:35–39).*

The call to repentance is sounded as an unquestionable sign of God's love (v. 19ff). The call is expressed in the language of the dinner host. This is the announcement of the parousia and is related to the parable of the servants waiting for their master (Lk 12:35–38), with the knocking, the opening by the servants, and the repast. This is the Messianic banquet theme, of which the Eucharist is an anticipation. Finally there is the enthronement. Just as the throne is given to Jesus by reason of his faithfulness and final victory (5:6), the same is extended to the faithful Christian.

Once again the churches are called to be attentive (v. 22).

THE MIDDLE GROUND

Tepidity. The word itself seems to betray its meaning. It's the cup of coffee that we have ordered, and the first sip confirms our fears. It's the hot compress that we apply to a swelling or an injury, and the absence of real heat makes it ineffectual. This was the problem at Laodicea, and when applied to our spiritual life, very few of us would be unaware of its meaning. Various types of Christian appear in this book of the Bible. In the face of vigorous opposition to Christianity, there were those who followed the Lord with genuine passion. Then there were those who just hung on, those to whom the word *commitment* meant very little. It was a question of "Come day, go day, God send Sunday." And we all know what that means.

There is probably some comfort in belonging without paying a price. One is neither fully "in" nor fully "out." Incredible excitement can be raised over a major league baseball game, a symphony concert, or an anticipated vacation. But when it comes to the great personal love story of Jesus the Christ, we often get a blank stare, or worse, a huge yawn. It is worthwhile at times to take a negative approach and ask ourselves what life would be like without Christianity. Suppose there were no message of hope, no teaching on the way to live, no God who cared about us passionately. Suppose there were no scriptures, no mass to attend, no baptism to be received. Life would be simply one huge gaping hole.

The Laodiceans had become so rich and affluent that they had forgotten how poor they were. It was pure deception. And if we insist on making created things the center of our lives, then we may be sure that Christ will be pushed to the periphery, still there, but not much. And as soon as Christian issues are introduced, our tepidity comes to the fore. From this indifferent state let us pray for deliverance. The only escape route is through love. If I really love and care, then I want to go the extra mile, my faith comes to life in service, and my Christianity makes a difference. But all of this can only happen when faith is nurtured through private prayer, reflection time, and a thoughtful weighing of eternal values.

THREE NECESSITIES

The people of Laodicea needed three things: fire-tested gold, white clothes, and eye ointment. Our faith too needs to be tested and burnished in the fire of trial, pain, and temptation. When we succeed in turning away from the path of evil because it is the right thing to do, faith is stronger, the gold is tested. God has won the day. If we can turn to people in real need and be truly present to them, then faith has come to life. Pain and hardship are distasteful, but there is no other way of testing our gold. In this way our riches will be real.

We also need the white clothing. It is the stain on the white shirt or the light skirt that irks us. Clothing is said to be the measure of the man, and many of us give it more than enough attention. In the moral order we are called to the same awareness. If we sin gravely, we know what to do. Genuine sorrow can make of any mishap "a happy fault." But tepidity simply wants to coexist with wrongdoing. It just doesn't matter that much, and so the tepid just go on wearing the stained shirt or the tattered blouse. When a faith response is no longer present and conviction counts for nothing, then we begin to move down that slippery slope of rejection of serious values. To turn away from evil vigorously requires energy, but some of us have become too portly to move that rapidly. So dalliance takes its place. TV channel surfing to find pornography. The beer-drinking companions who keep you at the bar until the late hours. At home with the people who delight in character assassination. Do we resist? Or follow the path of tepidity? If getting the stains out of our clothes means a trip to the cleaners, then let's be about it.

And finally, there is the ointment for the eyes. Francis of Assisi suffered from eye problems for much of his life. When he underwent very primitive eye surgery, he asked Brother Fire to treat him kindly and not add to his pain. And yet what spiritual vision he had. Part of our faith problem is the fact that we just don't see well. Perhaps we are not convinced of the reality that stands behind the words that we profess. Or our vision has become obscured by the daily hardship of providing for a family in economically difficult times. Or we are disturbed by all the turmoil in the church. Many things can obscure our faith vision, but the oil of healing is always there. Like the blind man in the gospel, we cry out, "Lord, grant that I may see." More people are touched by that healing grace than we imagine; it is not just wishful thinking. It came to Francis of Assisi while he was praying before a crucifix during a church visit. Dorothy Day stopped in a New York church for a little solitude, and she left on the path to faith. As we grow older we can tell when our eyes are going and cataracts are on the way. Reading becomes more difficult and less prolonged. That small print becomes an ever-greater annoyance. We know that the visit to the ophthalmologist cannot be delayed much longer. And yet what do we do about our blurring faith? Do we seek the ointment of a better, more mature understanding of our faith? Has my thinking changed since Vatican II? When was my last retreat? My last confession? Do I turn to the scriptures? Find ways to understand them better? Will it be balm for the eyes or continued tepidity?

And yet the master, the host of the Messianic banquet, never gives up on us. All too many people have given up on themselves. Damaged goods are labeled irreparable. Yet who wants to continue to be lackluster, spiritually dull, a "blip" on the radar screen. It is equivalent to the person who settles before the TV screen, with beer and pretzels, consigned to the life of a "couch potato." How different it is with Christ, the hound of heaven who pursues us down the nights and down the days. He stands at the door and knocks, and all we have to do is to open it. That one image in Revelation of Christ at the door conjures up countless scenarios in the Gospels: Christ at table with sinners, Christ with the crowds, the children, the disconsolate. The Christ who never tires.

We can only be grateful that God does not act as we do. We who give up after the second or third knock. How often have we said, "Yes, I'll keep in touch," and then don't. "Absence makes the heart grow fonder" eventually becomes "out of sight, out of mind." But not so with Christ. He is always there, ready and willing to forgive, offering the invitation anew. This is such a powerful message of the Gospels; it brings boundless consolation. In the midst of sinfulness and discouragement, of tepidity and half-hearted response, there is always the God who saves, the Christ who remains the same yesterday, today, and forever. He gives us life, limitless forgiveness, and, at any moment in our troubled existence, stands at the door and knocks.

Lukewarmness at Laodicea

1. Do you see a fair measure of tepid Christianity with us today?

2. Do we appreciate the examination of conscience?

3. Why is there so much difficulty with lifetime commitments today?

4. In Laodicea there was gold, clothing, and eye ointments. Can these be useful metaphors for aspects of our life today?

5. How do you experience "lukewarmness" in your own life? How do you deal with it?

II. JUDGMENT ON THE EVIL EMPIRE (4:1–18:24)

GOD AND THE LAMB IN HEAVEN (4:1–11)

4:1 After this I had a vision of an open door to heaven, and I heard the trumpetlike voice that had spoken to me before, saying, "Come up here and I will show you what must happen afterwards."

4:2 At once I was caught up in spirit. A throne was there in heaven, and on the throne sat

4:3 one whose appearance sparkled like jasper and carnelian. Around the throne was a halo as brilliant as an emerald.

4:4 Surrounding the throne I saw twenty-four other thrones on which twenty-four elders sat, dressed in white garments and with gold crowns on their heads.

4:5 From the throne came flashes of lightning, rumblings, and peals of thunder. Seven flaming torches burned in front of the throne, which are the seven spirits of God.

4:6 In front of the throne was something that resembled a sea of glass like crystal. In the center and around the throne, there were four living creatures covered with eyes in front and in back.

4:7 The first creature resembled a lion, the second was like a calf, the third had a face like that of a human being, and the fourth looked like an eagle in flight.

4:8 The four living creatures, each of them with six wings, were covered with eyes inside and out. Day and night they do not stop exclaiming:
"Holy, holy, holy is the Lord God almighty,
who was, and who is, and who is to come."

4:9 Whenever the living creatures give glory and honor and thanks to the one who sits on the throne, who lives forever and ever,

4:10 the twenty-four elders fall down before the one who sits on the throne and worship him, who lives forever and ever. They throw down their crowns before the throne, exclaiming:

4:11 "Worthy are you, Lord our God,
to receive glory and honor and power,
for you created all things;
because of your will they came to be and were created."

At this point we move into the distinctly revelatory part of the book, the visions of the heavenly court, the things that are to come. The chapter begins with the phrase "After this" in order to move us beyond the difficulties of the present time, seen in the first three chapters, toward considerations of the end time, characterized by two distinct phases: eschatological distress and beatific outcome. There is, of course, continuity between the present, with its trials and hardships, and the end that stands on the horizon; but there is also discontinuity as the seer transposes his message into an unearthly key characterized by signs and symbols. This should not be read sequentially; it is not a question of "before" and "after." The heavenly vision stands outside of time, embracing past, present, and future. Much remains to be made known, or better, to be revealed. This will occur only with the breaking of the seals.

There is a majestic sweep to the opening vision, which should be looked at as a whole before addressing individual parts. The vision emerges through an open door, which leads into the heavenly vault. The throne is the centerpiece surrounded by attendants in a variety of forms: the seven torches of fire, the four living creatures, the twenty-four elders on twenty-four thrones. Notice that the occupant of the throne is left undefined, except in terms of blinding light and incredible brilliance. The climactic moment comes when praise is sung to the one God.

The imagery of this chapter draws heavily on the first chapter of

Ezekiel, with the presence of other theophany elements (e.g., Ex 19). This is seen in the throne, the living creatures, the rainbow-like halo, the thunder and lightning.

• The throne *(v. 2): The jewel-like precious stones sparkle about the throne. The absence of any figure on the throne underscores the transcendence of God.*

• Twenty-four elders on twenty-four thrones *(v. 4): The enthroned elders signify authority, related to the Sovereign's earthly reign. They represent the twelve tribes of Israel and the twelve apostles. This underscores the comprehensive character of the Sovereign's domain, embracing both covenants; and it is total in its scope, touching heaven and earth. They have royal authority (crowns) and innocence and uprightness of life (white garments), the latter also symbolizing loyalty even to martyrdom if necessary (7:13f).*

• Seven flaming torches *(v. 5): These represent the seven spirits of God. They are the messengers of God, in some way an extension of his person. They are part of the throne room's furnishings (torches, attendants at the throne), are sent out into the world, and represent God's omniscience and guidance (eyes of God).*

• Four living creatures *(v. 6): These are drawn from Ezekiel 1 but are described differently. The eyes in front and back give them oversight, knowledge, and direction. The image connected with each (lion, ox, human, and eagle) point to the supremacy of God over all creation, especially its noblest species. A Jewish midrash reads: "Man is exalted among creatures, the eagle among birds, the ox among domestic animals, the lion among wild beasts; all of them have received dominion." Thus, each is a preferred category, an elevated species in the created order. Yet God is sovereign over them all. They are at his command. The wings are those of the seraphim (Is 6:2). At a later date in Christian tradition the four creatures will be identified with the evangelists: Mark, Luke, Matthew, and John respectively.*

• Sea of glass like crystal *(v. 6): Here there are shades of the crystal firmament (Ez 1:26), coupled with late Judaism's belief in a vast sea that was part of the heavenly realm. The sea is devoid of any chaotic characteristics; rather it is tranquil and as smooth and transparent as glass.*

• The choruses *(vv. 8–11): Praise by the four living creatures is constant and represents the praise of all creation; thematically it centers on God's eternity, his lordship* (kyrios) *and omnipotence* (pantokrator). *The praise from the twenty-four elders has them recognize their subordinate authority (casting down their crowns) and praising God emphatically as the creator of all that is.*

What we have here is a dramatic and impressive acknowledgment of God's sovereignty over the whole of history (the twenty-four elders), the whole of creation (the four creatures) and the heavenly beings (the seven spirits). God is brought into direct relationship with the whole created order, thus overcoming any dualism or Gnostic rejection of creation.

HONOR AND PRAISE

There is something almost operatic about the sweeping grandeur of this opening scene of the enthroned God and his worshipers. We have all experienced something akin to this in the theater when the curtain rises on a breathtaking spectacle. Yahweh is not seen; only his appurtenances are visible, yet he remains the centerpiece, effulgent and splendid, whose radiance envelops the entire scene. The surrounding court remains wholly centered on the main figure, as they address their praise to him. Everything is artfully and skillfully depicted as centripetal, as the four living creatures and the twenty-four elders acclaim the one enthroned as Lord and Creator.

Worship stands at the center and apogee of our lives as Christians. We perform no nobler task. We begin where the worshipers of chapter 4 begin, with God in and for himself, the one who out of sheer goodness and no duress created the universe that surrounds us and each one of us as well. It is within that framework of the eternal and good God that we will subsequently place the redeeming Christ, who is simply a further expression of God's goodness.

The Vatican Council gave as much attention to Christian worship as to any other item on its agenda. It was the first document of the Council to be ratified and published. It set a whole new tone for worship and for what it means to pray. Liturgical prayer has priority of place because it is the church at prayer. It is raised out of the sphere of personal devotion and becomes the finest expression of what we as a church are all about. Perhaps it is best appreciated by those who have spanned the years before, during, and after.

There is no doubting the fact that the pre–Vatican II mass had a very sacred quality, enshrined as it was in silence, an ancient language, a great musical tradition, incense, and bells. With all the discussion pro and con, we cannot underestimate its value in enhancing our relationship with God. While active participation was minimal, even though encouraged, the Latin mass succeeded in another way, in helping us appreciate the transcendence of God and our concurrent responsibility. Its supporters are still vocal at this point, many years after the Council. There is great question as to whether it will survive, if for no other reason than that two generations have arisen who simply do not know the former liturgy at all. It would be sad if it were to remain only as a symbolic statement for retrenching Catholics, since that is not the role liturgy is called to play.

To its lasting credit, the former liturgy was a very vital vehicle of prayer. Certainly many people did not understand Latin and could not have explained the sense of every prayer that was said, but it succeeded admirably in relating the aesthetical to the holy, of lifting the human spirit to something and someone beyond. At its best it succeeded remarkably well, which is not to say that it could not be offered in a mediocre and uninspiring way. For many people, however, it was a source of conviction and strength.

THE DAWN OF CHANGE

More than in any other area, the effects of Vatican II were profoundly felt in worship. Seminary life in those turning-point years was very interesting. The students of those days were ready for change, and each session of the Council brought more. To be a seminary professor or administrator meant "corking" boundless enthusiasm and "reining in" the strong and urgent desire to move the agenda forward. In the earliest stages the position of the altar was changed, a limited amount of English was introduced, concelebration was reintroduced. Texts were in an almost constant state of flux as more and more vernacular was introduced. In retrospect, it seems that we were much more involved in the mechanics of change rather than its underlying spirit. But before too much time passed, there was the realization that much more basic work had to be done, and we saw the introduction of liturgy as a major theological course. Prior to that time, liturgy had simply been rubrics. We learned how to baptize, marry, anoint, and bury. Now the theology of worship was emerging, as well as the history of the rites we celebrate. This was a great breath of fresh air.

One wonders if anywhere, except in the Catholic Church, such sweeping change could be accepted and implemented over such a short period of time with as little fallout as there was. Catholics had long been used to an unquestioning acceptance of decisions by authority, and this proved itself in the wake of the Vatican Council. Some people were enthusiastic about change; others were not but believed in the church's right to so act. And honesty compels us to admit in hindsight that much of the change was implemented in a very uneven fashion. In countless cases there was insufficient catechesis, with little understanding of the rationale behind the changes. Churches were redesigned in an unthinking manner. A musical patrimony of centuries was set aside, and the substitute was initially quite inferior. But change we did, and it must be admitted that there was more that was positive than negative.

With Vatican II, we passed from prayerful attendance at mass to being true offerers. The paradigm shift was enormous, even if many did not understand it. Active participation improved continually as previously quiet Catholics learned to sing and pray aloud. New ministries brought the common priesthood of believers very much to the fore. The sanctuary, once the almost exclusive domain of the priest, was now peopled with lectors, cantors, servers, and eucharistic ministers. The sense of community was enhanced by the design of new churches, which united the faithful in proximity to the sanctuary and the altar. The scripture was opened much more abundantly, with many books of the Bible read on Sundays and weekdays throughout the year. Gradually there was a renewal of the rites of all the sacraments as we moved forward in a new era of church life.

On the positive side, it must be said that this has made a great difference in our life of faith. The liturgical changes of the Council and the follow-up to those changes represent the culmination of close to a century of study and scholarship. In many ways we were ready for change. We now stand on soil that has been freshly tilled and sown. The full benefits have yet to be reaped.

And this is where Revelation can shed light on our efforts. All worship, and indeed all prayer, must center on the Lord alone. There is no group in the image we have examined that does not have its attention riveted on Yahweh. Their proclamation of "Holy, holy, holy" reminds us that God always belongs to the realm of the other, which is what Hebrew holiness truly means. Our catechesis must return to this point repeatedly, the worship of the God of heaven and earth, if our efforts are not to be reduced to mere mechanics, going through the motions. We can end up with perfect order and still remain uninspiring. And this is where balance is so necessary. While we want to enhance the closeness of God, the humanity of Christ, and the human dimension of worship, we must be equally strong in a cult that relates to the transcendent, to that which is clearly not commonplace, to the sanctity of God.

REVERENCE

Therefore, we must be constantly renewed in spirit. If the liturgy is offered hurriedly, with no silence or time for reverence, or if the celebration is offered in an inaudible or uninspiring tone of voice, or with a homily hardly worthy of the name, what have we gained? If lay ministers at the altar are not reverent, properly attired, or inaccurately designated "bread and wine ministers," can we be said to be in tune with the meaning of liturgy? If lectors read poorly and cannot be understood and yet continue in their position interminably, is the Word really being proclaimed? When children, and not infrequently adults as well, receive the Eucharist so hurriedly, as they take, eat, and head back to their pews without losing a beat, in what sense can this be said to be an expression of faith?

The Council said wisely that liturgical prayer and private prayer dovetail beautifully. And it would seem that if the great liturgical riches derived from the Council are to be ours, then they must be accompanied by a prayerful spirit, a true sense of the meaning of "silence" and "alone." *Sancta sanctis.* Holy things for holy people. The restored liturgy reminds us of our position before God and our responsibility to the world. As a priestly people, we know that social action is closely related to the Eucharist, as is all our involvement in the world. But this is related to spirituality, and there is nothing automatic about our life in God. It involves interpreting symbol, listening to and contemplating the Word, especially silent reflection. "Holy, holy, holy is the Lord God almighty."

Thinking about Liturgy

1. What do you think of the place of drama, art, and music in religious experience?

2. Can you define a theophany?

3. Do we see the liturgy as the noblest form of prayer?

4. Theology says, "The law of praying is the law of believing." What is its meaning?

5. The reign of God points to the sovereignty of God over all of creation. Concretely, how do we interpret that?

6. Are you at ease with apocalyptic imagery?

THE LAMB AND THE SCROLL (5:1–14)

5:1 **I saw a scroll in the right hand of the one who sat on the throne. It had writing on both sides and was sealed with seven seals.**

5:2 **Then I saw a mighty angel who proclaimed in a loud voice, "Who is worthy to open the scroll and break its seals?"**

5:3 **But no one in heaven or on earth or under the earth was able to open the scroll or to examine it.**

5:4 **I shed many tears because no one was found worthy to open the scroll or to examine it.**

5:5 One of the elders said to me, "Do not weep. The lion of the tribe of Judah, the root of David, has triumphed, enabling him to open the scroll with its seven seals."

5:6 Then I saw standing in the midst of the throne and the four living creatures and the elders, a Lamb that seemed to have been slain. He had seven horns and seven eyes; these are the (seven) spirits of God sent out into the whole world.

5:7 He came and received the scroll from the right hand of the one who sat on the throne.

5:8 When he took it, the four living creatures and the twenty-four elders fell down before the Lamb. Each of the elders held a harp and gold bowls filled with incense, which are the prayers of the holy ones.

5:9 They sang a new hymn:
"Worthy are you to receive the scroll
 and to break open its seals,
for you were slain and with your blood you purchased for
God
those from every tribe and tongue, people and nation.

5:10 You made them a kingdom and priests for our God,
and they will reign on earth."

5:11 I looked again and heard the voices of many angels who surrounded the throne and the living creatures and the elders. They were countless in number,

5:12 and they cried out in a loud voice:
"Worthy is the Lamb that was slain
to receive power and riches, wisdom and strength,
honor and glory and blessing."

5:13 Then I heard every creature in heaven and on earth and under the earth and in the sea, everything in the universe, cry out:
"To the one who sits on the throne and to the Lamb
be blessing and honor, glory and might,
forever and ever."

5:14 The four living creatures answered, "Amen," and the elders fell down and worshiped.

Mystery surrounds the initial emergence of the Lamb, the Christ of glory. It is important to note that the Lamb is actually superimposed over the One seated upon the throne (vv. 1,6); they blend together yet remain distinct.

To Christ the victor belongs the right to take the scroll, which contains the "end time" denouement, *the unfolding of the final events known only to God, marked profoundly by punishment for sin and injustice. By reason of his victory over sin and death, Christ alone outlines the divine picture of the final days.* Seven seals *(v. 1): The seals were used to authenticate a document; that there were seven of them points to completeness or the definitive character of what is predicted. The intermediate weeping (v. 4) is a dramatic delay in the execution of the plan in order to place the Lamb in sharper relief.* Lion of the tribe of Judah *(v. 5): The davidic Messiah (Gn 49:9–11).* The root of Jesse *(v. 5): Again, the davidic line is noted, Jesse being the father of David (Is 11:1).*

However, the lion quickly fades into the image of the lamb. This is a rich pastoral designation. It draws on the passover lamb (Ex 12), whose blood became an agent of deliverance, and the innocent lamb led to slaughter in the fourth song of the Servant (Is 53:7). The Lamb image appears frequently in Revelation (twenty-nine times), but the qualification here has particular importance: it is the Lamb who has been slain *(v. 6). The use of the participle in the perfect tense* (Gr.: esphagmenon) *points to a permanent and lasting sign of suffering. The suffering of Christ has been incorporated into his resurrection. The lion–lamb imagery speaks of strength in weakness, the great scandal of the cross, "a stumbling block to Jews and foolishness to Gentiles." Yet ironically Christ is "the power of God and the wisdom of God" (1 Cor 1:22–24).* Seven horns...seven eyes *(v. 6): The former express the power, the latter the wisdom of God, both related to the seven spirits of God, which look to his all pervading presence in the universe. Omnipotence, omniscience, omnipresence–all expressions of the one God. It is not difficult to see trinitarian implications in this picture of the Eternal One, the Lamb, and the spirits.*

The scene is climaxed by the acceptance of the scroll (v. 7), all of which is geared to the recognition of the Lamb's preeminence by the elders, the four living creatures, the countless angels (literally, thousands upon thousands; v. 11), and finally the whole of the universe (v. 13).

The First Hymn (vv. 9–10)

In this short hymn the homage and recognition due the Lamb are not based on eternal preeminence but rather on his redemptive work. Every tribe and tongue *(v. 9): Salvation is universal.* Kingdom and priests *(v. 10): The Christians already constitute a reign, as participants in Christ's victory through baptism. As priests they share in Christ's mediating role between God and the world, which is proper to the common priesthood of the faithful (1 Pt 2:6; Ex 19:6).*

The Second Hymn (v. 12)

There are seven attributes given to the Lamb. The first four (power, riches, wisdom, and strength) are proper to God in himself and are expressive of sovereignty and dominion. The last three (honor, glory, and blessing) look to the response to be given to the Sovereign by his subjects (4:9).

The Third Hymn (v. 13)

Here praise comes from all of creation. It is directed to God and Christ (the Lamb) and is perpetual. Hebrew cosmogony comes to the fore in the "three-decker" world (above, center, and below) as well as the sea, a threatening locale (13:1; 21:1), the dwelling place of the sea monsters, Rahab and Leviathan. We have here a cosmic Christology, not unlike that of Colossians 1, but without a pre-existent or creating Christ. Here attention is centered on the redemptive Christ. The final "Amen" and prostration (v. 14) is a striking attestation of the sovereignty of God and the lordship of Jesus. The chapter ends on a note of victory already achieved and yet a process still to be unfolded in the chapters that follow. The final struggle is still to be experienced. And chapter 6 marks its beginning.

THE LAMB AND THE KINGDOM OF PRIESTS

Enter the Lamb....Nothing is more distinctive of Christianity than its humanity. This embraces the Hebrew tradition with its God of engagement and his tender grasp of a people, but in a special way, with God's clothing himself in humanness in the person of Jesus. This becomes remarkably clear at this point in Revelation as the glorified Lamb is inserted deeply into the picture of the heavenly court, which acclaims God in his transcendent majesty. In a certain sense, the extraneous and unlikely move front and center. And it is the Lamb "that seemed to have been slain," with signs of its bloody death all too evident. Not only is humanity acknowledged, but the human in its beaten, abused, and rejected form. As incongruous as it seems, if we truly weigh the image, it is this wounded animal that receives the acclaim reserved to God alone. If we were not so anesthetized to this monumental leap, we would be truly astounded.

Let us step back a bit. In the Gospels, various titles are given to Jesus that represent the early church's recognition of his status: Messiah, Savior, Lord, Servant. How many of these go back to the time of Jesus' earthly ministry is not easy to say. But what is clear is the difficulty experienced in earliest Christianity in according Jesus the title God. When the young man approaches Jesus in Mark's Gospel and refers to him as "good," Jesus corrects the man immediately and rejects the compliment because "No one is good but God alone" (Mk 10:18). Since Yahweh alone was God (in an exclusively monotheistic religion), it was clear that whoever Jesus was he was not Yahweh. It is only with the passing of time that the risen Christ is accorded the exclusive appellative proper to God alone. As the relationship of Christ to God became clearer, accompanied by the realization that *God* is a more inclusive term, the scriptures clearly state that the Word (Jesus) is not only with God but is God (Jn 1:1).

This makes the proximity of the Lamb to the One enthroned in Revelation a matter of particular interest. There is a unity and diversity present here. And it is found in a cultic setting. It was in worship that the doctrinal implications related to the Trinity emerged early on. It is due to the fact that Jesus is being worshiped as Lord at an early period that doctrine begins to emerge.

Lex orandi, lex credendi. Prayer and faith are one. Since the term *Lord* was a surrogate for the unpronounced name *Yahweh,* the fact that it is accorded to Christ in early liturgical expression (Phil 2:11) indicates that we are on the road to a full recognition of divinity. In the light of his death-resurrection, Jesus was not simply a rabbi, a wonder worker, or even simply Messiah. He belonged to the realm of God, and the ways to express that reality became known only by degrees. Worship was one of the principal avenues of clarification.

In Roman literature early Christians were spoken of as praying "to their Christ as to a god." It was the lamb who had been slain, but slain for all peoples of all times. He and the One enthroned are now one in bringing reconciliation to the entire world, people of every "tribe, tongue, and nation." Two overwhelming thoughts come to mind. First, we acknowledge this Nazarean carpenter, this man who suffered from fatigue, hunger, and discouragement, the one who hung naked in total humiliation on a cross before a jeering crowd, as our deity, our Lord, the one who is co-responsible for all that is beautiful and good, the one who presides over history, the one who is eternal.

Second, if this is true, then we can never again say that God doesn't understand. He knows what it is to be human. Suffering and death will always be shrouded in mystery, and humanly we will always shrink from them. But we do see them in a different light. In one of Rod Serling's dramas on the early TV series *The Twilight Zone,* an elderly woman living alone is afraid to die. She lives in a basement apartment where she is beset by anxiety, until a young man comes and befriends her. He becomes the recipient of her total trust and confidence. One day he asks her to leave her apartment and come with him. With trusting eyes she looks up at him and says, "Yes." She puts her hand in his; he takes her arm and they leave. The final scene reverts to her apartment where she lies dead on her bed. The message is strikingly Christian. It is hard to pray to a God who is somewhere "out there." We turn to the God who touches us in Christ, takes our hand when there is fear, and gives us the assurance that "he has been there himself." If we but realized the gift that is ours!

ROYALTY

He has made of us "a kingdom and priests." The expression is a paraphrase of a quote from Exodus 19, wherein the Israelites are termed a "kingdom of priests." We are not used to thinking of ourselves as royalty, and we probably shouldn't. But the fact is that the kingdom of God is here, and we are all part of it. It is all in the Spirit, of course, but it speaks volumes about our personal worth.

It is as true of the affluent suburbanite as it is of the poor tribals of northern India who put their "little"—a few eggs and some rice—in the collection basket at Sunday Mass. Baptism clothes each one of us in radiant splendor. We have put on the living Christ in his Holy Spirit. That having been said, nothing can go too wrong. We may become despondent but are never desperate, rejected but never alone. The kingdom is so identified with joy in the scriptures that only eating and drinking will do. It is the new and the best of wines, the choice meats, the wedding feast, merry-making, dancing, and laughter. Even Jesus said that there is no time for fasting when celebration is the order of the day.

We are so beset by problems that there seems to be little real joy. We hear much about celebration—the Mass, the sacraments—but experience all too little. The church, a center of controversy, offers too little change for some and too much for others. There is no doubt that many of us would like things to be different, but the essentials are always there, and that has to give us cause for joy. We reign in the kingdom of God, and we can never forget it.

...AND PRIESTS

But we are also priests. Priesthood has become a revered institution in Catholic life. And there is much thinking today about where it is headed. While recognizing the importance the ordained priesthood has attained in Catholic life, it is interesting to note that the term *priest* in the New Testament is used only in reference to Christ (in Hebrews) and to the faithful as a whole (in 1 Peter). Here in Revelation it is applied to those who are part of the kingdom. And so we are all priests by doing what priests do. They are mediators between God and the world. They bring the prayers and concerns of their people and the world at large to the sanctuary. They are the designated intercessors for a people in need, for those who often go unheard, for the forgotten. Prayer stands at the very heart of their life.

Moreover, as mediators they also bring God *to* people. They share the scriptures, they visit the sick, they minister the Eucharist, they are agents of consolation. They are the gentle hands of God in touch, the voice of God in consoling speech, the feet of God in being messengers of peace. But above all, they mirror God in a godless world. They live their lives in such a way that they would make no sense if God did not exist. They live by values that are deeply rooted in God. In this way they bring God to the world. They forgive the unforgivable because of the father of the prodigal son. They are merciful because Christ asked for mercy. They remain husband and wife, even when the seas are stormy, because that is what the Christ of the gospels requests. They turn the other cheek, go the extra mile, lend without interest, and give without counting the cost. They are priests of the living God. This is the priesthood of the faithful.

And so in this age of a shortage of priests and an absence of kings, we have more of both than we ever imagined. It is the woman in the south Bronx who spends her days seeing that the needs of the homebound are met. It is the suburban couple who are involved in a parish census, trying to reach the unchurched. It is the young caregiver, so unfamiliar with death, who stays beside a dying AIDS patient for months on end. It is the elderly gentleman who lights the candle in church on behalf of someone in need. And it is the old Irish friar who on a long trip likes to say one more rosary every five hundred miles for someone else in need. They are all priests, and in the kingdom which is theirs they shall reign forever.

Interpreting Symbols

1. Three images appear in this chapter: the One enthroned, the Lamb, and the seven spirits. What does this suggest to you? Are there trinitarian implications?

2. Do you have trouble understanding the sovereignty of Christ in a secular world?

3. Christ is both lion and lamb in chapter 5. How can both images be applied to Christ?

4. "The lamb who was slain" points to the permanent signs of Christ's suffering. How do we explain the image?

5. Do we ever think of a church choir reflecting a heavenly choir giving continuous praise to God?

6. Today theology speaks of "the cosmic Christ." What meaning does that have for you?

THE BEGINNING OF THE GREAT TRIBULATION
THE FIRST SIX SEALS (6:1–17)

6:1 Then I watched while the Lamb broke open the first of the seven seals, and I heard one of the four living creatures cry out in a voice like thunder, "Come forward."

6:2 I looked, and there was a white horse, and its rider had a bow. He was given a crown, and he rode forth victorious to further his victories.

6:3 When he broke open the second seal, I heard the second living creature cry out, "Come forward."

6:4 Another horse came out, a red one. Its rider was given power to take peace away from the earth, so that people would slaughter one another. And he was given a huge sword.

6:5 When he broke open the third seal, I heard the third living creature cry out, "Come forward." I looked, and there was a black horse, and its rider held a scale in his hand.

6:6 I heard what seemed to be a voice in the midst of the four living creatures. It said, "A ration of wheat costs a day's pay, and three rations of barley cost a day's pay. But do not damage the olive oil or the wine."

6:7 When he broke open the fourth seal, I heard the voice of the fourth living creature cry out, "Come forward."

6:8 I looked, and there was a pale green horse. Its rider was named Death, and Hades accompanied him. They were given authority over a quarter of the earth, to kill with sword, famine, and plague, and by means of the beasts of the earth.

6:9 When he broke open the fifth seal, I saw underneath the altar the souls of those who had been slaughtered because of the witness they bore to the word of God.

6:10 They cried out in a loud voice, "How long will it be, holy and true master, before you sit in judgment and avenge our blood on the inhabitants of the earth?"

6:11 Each of them was given a white robe, and they were told to be patient a little while longer until the number was filled of their fellow servants and brothers who were going to be killed as they had been.

6:12 Then I watched while he broke open the sixth seal, and there was a great earthquake; the sun turned as black as dark sackcloth and the whole moon became like blood.

6:13 The stars in the sky fell to the earth like unripe figs shaken loose from the tree in a strong wind.

6:14 Then the sky was divided like a torn scroll curling up, and every mountain and island was moved from its place.

6:15 The kings of the earth, the nobles, the military officers, the rich, the powerful, and every slave and free person hid themselves in caves and among mountain crags.

6:16 They cried out to the mountains and the rocks, "Fall on us and hide us from the face of the one who sits on the throne and from the wrath of the Lamb,

6:17 because the great day of their wrath has come and who can withstand it?"

The woes of the final period will find expression in the seals (c. 6), the trumpets (cc. 8–9), and the bowls (cc. 16–18). The Old Testament background

to the seals is found in Zechariah 1:8–10, 6:1–8. The unconnected sequence in the narrative of the scrolls has three moments: the seal is opened, a voice is heard, and a horse appears.

The privilege of unsealing an official document, like the opening of an envelope, belonged only to the one properly designated. This belongs to Christ, who by reason of his redemptive death has been awarded complete and total sovereignty (v. 1; 5:9).

The First Seal (vv. 1–2)

The white horse and rider are symbols of imperial warfare, the invasion of a foreign power, a possible reference to the victory of the Parthian invaders over the Romans in A.D. 62. Whatever the background, the image here becomes symbolic and eschatological; the victory of the invader over his enemy symbolizes the calamity before the end.

The Second Seal (vv. 3–4)

The picture is one of general panic. The red stands for blood; the sword, for slaughter (Ez 21:14–17). Rather than an invasion, we are faced with internal insurrection with mutual killing. Peace is withdrawn from the earth, in much the same way as the peace of Eden is destroyed by the sin (Gn 1–3), which then finds concrete expression in the killing of Abel (Gn 4). What is true of the beginning is true of the end as wanton slaughter comes to the fore (cf. Mk 13:8).

The Third Seal (vv. 5–6)

Famine emerges with the fourth seal's opening (Lv 26:26; Ez 4:16f). The scale (v.5): Symbol of rationing. A day's pay (v.6): Literally, a denarius, the usual stipend for a day's work. The point is that wheat and barley, the basic staples of daily life, are going at exorbitant prices. A glimmer of hope remains, however, with wine and oil remaining untouched. It is a dire picture of famine and impoverishment.

The Fourth Seal (vv. 7–8)

This plague is death itself. The rider is so named, and he is accompanied by Hades, the underworld, or Sheol, the realm of the dead. This matches the contemporary image of the Grim Reaper! The accompanying images are an overlay of what has already been presented as the end-time lot–war, slaughter, and famine (Ez 14:21)–but again there are limits placed on destruction, with only a fourth of humanity being destroyed.

The Fifth Seal (vv. 9–11)

Souls *(v. 9)* (Gr.: psychai): *This is a clear expression of the immortal human principle independent of the resurrected body. The martyrs had died under Roman persecution. The location under the altar relates them to sacrifice, that of Christ and their own. Life was in the blood in Hebrew thought (Lv 17:11), and the blood of animal victims was gathered at the base of the altar. However, their distress still continues as they cry out for the vindication of God's justice. This is not vengeance but vindication that is requested; only through exoneration will the record be set straight and end-time justice served.* Holy and true master *(v.10): Probably addressed to God, not Christ, the designation points to his otherness and covenant fidelity.*

The time of persecution is not yet over (v. 11), but they are already numbered among the elect, as indicated by the white robe, the symbol of their permanent and unending inheritance (Mt 22:11–14).

The fifth seal underscores the fact that the entire end-time scenario is in God's hands and remains always under his direction.

The Sixth Seal (vv. 12–16)

No end-time picture would be complete without cosmic upheaval, and with the sixth seal it is unleashed with full force. This is a true Götterdämmerung! *We have:*
- Earthquake (Jl 2:10; Is 24:9)
- Discolored sun and moon (Mt 24:29; Is 13:10, 50:3; Jl 3:4)
- Collapsing firmament and falling stars (Is 34:4). *With the*

stars affixed to the heavenly firmament like ornaments, when one falls, so does the other.

All peoples of the earth, regardless of rank or station, hide themselves from the final judgment (vv. 15–17; Is 2:10, 19). This end of time scenario is imaging the unimaginable, and this must always be kept in mind when interpreting apocalyptic literature if literalism is not to hold sway. No one is given an inside track on what will take place, yet the six seals all point to the destruction and passing of the present order in the face of the new order to be established.

THE ERA OF THE TRAGIC

Both the One enthroned and the Lamb pass from the scene when the utter destruction is introduced with the opening of the six seals. It is the Lamb who breaks the seals, but he remains removed from the events that follow. Evil must have its day before final victory emerges; indeed it has been an ingredient of salvation history from the earliest pages of Genesis. That inherent freedom that comes from being human must allow for right and wrong, for good and evil, as the denouement of history makes eminently clear. While making no attempt at pinpointing the end of time, we would have to admit that the imagery of the six seals has taken on astounding actuality in the final century of the second millennium. And God has been as absent from what has occurred, sometimes bewilderingly so, as he is in the events that transpire in this chapter of Revelation. The surreal imagery, with its various manifestations of ugliness, is reflective of the incredible pain and inhumanity that has been inflicted upon millions of people in the past hundred years. The teaching on evil has been given a human face. It does little good to look at Revelation in the abstract, with a meaning that lies somewhere ahead of us, and fail to perceive its lesson in the here and now of our own historical experience.

INVASION

The white horse, the symbol of an invading power, certainly had meaning for the Roman Empire, with its expanding and vulnerable borders, just as the white horse of the first seal was reminiscent of the type of expansion that Rome itself had perpetrated. *Lebensraum* was the deceptive excuse proffered by Nazi Germany in the 1930s to explain its military exploits throughout Europe. "Living room" was needed to provide for an ever-increasing population. A military invasion brings its own type of terror. It is wanton destruction, rape, and theft; it is domination and control at its worst. I remember being in the city of Aachen, talking with German citizens who remembered vividly the Nazi invasion of Holland. They spoke of the troops and tanks amassed along the border the night before the invasion, poised to strike a lethal blow leading to swift capitulation, at the same time as Hitler was broadcasting a deceptive message to the Dutch people, a message of endearment and nonaggression. The multiple invasions of World War II subjugated a large part of Europe to a foreign yoke.

The incursion of North Korea upon the South brought years of untold hardship. It ended with the same division of the country that had obtained before it began. And the litany goes on and on. Vietnam, Iraq, Bosnia. Political and military entanglements that make it almost impossible to sort out the truth heap nothing but misery and hardship upon the innocent victims of war. Invasion has meant massive deportation with no idea of destination; it has meant indiscriminate killing, theft, and the wholesale raping of women. Yet how quickly this becomes a statistic read in the morning newspaper, or a short film clip on the evening news. But the fact remains that this is the real life of real people, with their faces etched in pain. And how many times we have been witnesses in the century that has passed! It is a case of Apocalypse Now.

DEADLY REPRISAL

The rider of the red horse is an agent of mutual slaughter. People destroy one another. In modern history this, too, has become all too common. It ranges from tribal wars in Africa to ethnic cleansing in the Balkans. It conjures up images of the "killing fields" in Cambodia with their endless rows of empty skulls. Or it brings to mind the death camps where the vanquished were lined up in early morning, transported by truck to an isolated spot, blindfolded, made to kneel, and summarily shot and buried in an open grave. Regardless of where the fault may lie, neither war nor death is a solution to human ills. It simply means artillery poised to kill, bombings that cannot be described as discriminate, children in flight aflame with napalm. Fantasy cannot outdo actuality when it comes to the frightening forms that human hatred can take.

The two coincide: apocalyptic language and the experience of human history. Some would feel that we have already experienced our apocalypse. But the one lesson to be learned is this: How contrary all of this is to the authentic spirit of Jesus. Peaceful resolution of difficulties, forgiveness, and humility stand in striking contrast to belligerence, hatred, and killing. We have witnessed Christians fighting Christians, both sides invoking God's blessing upon their military endeavor. How deceived we are! How far we have to journey in bringing a truly Christian spirit to life. A sobering thought indeed.

HUNGER

The third horse is a black stallion, announcing famine as part of the final experience. Hunger in the world seems almost inconceivable in an age of plenty and technological expertise. The absence of food sufficient for basic nutrition contrasts so strikingly with the abundance that is present in some parts of the world. In this day and age it seems impossible that people should die for want of food, and yet it happens repeatedly. The images remain lodged in our psyche: the children with enlarged stomachs and bulging eyes; the mothers' breasts that have no more milk to give; the hard and rocky earth, lifeless and barren, symbolic of final disaster; people collecting blades of grass to eat.

It is incorrect to say that the affluent world is indifferent to hunger; the response is generous and heartfelt. Humanitarian agencies work desperately to bring aid directly to people, often thwarted in their efforts by bureaucracy or corruption in the receiving country. And yet this does not remove the basic inequality. The meaning of famine in the wake of the black horse's advent should not be lost on us. Starving masses should not be present in a world of advanced technology and resources to cope with the problem. The means are there to assure fertile soil and to predict food shortages well in advance. The whole question of adjusting the world economy is painfully slow in effective solutions. Many visits to India in years past left me with the indelible memory of tribal people who lived on one bowl of rice each day. We are told repeatedly that starvation can be overcome and that famine need not occur. The Bible tells us that hunger is to be overcome: Joseph in Egypt, the manna in the desert, Elijah and the impoverished widow, Jesus with the loaves and fishes. There is an important lesson in the third seal that goes well beyond apocalyptic imagery.

DEATH

With the breaking of the fourth seal, the pale green horse signals the advent of death, the last word in evil's realm. Death is accompanied by its long-time biblical companion, Sheol, the place of final consignment. Sin, death, and Sheol symbolize alienation from God, the arena where God is absent and evil holds sway. Death is always a difficult reality. Every person must face it alone in making the final solitary journey. When it touches another, closeness or intimacy will determine the extent of our grief. When it comes in a tragic form, it can have a devastating effect. In the forms represented by the fourth seal, once again mutual killing and natural disaster come to the fore. Memories from modern history flash in our minds: blindfolded prisoners being shot in the base of the skull; people being herded into "shower rooms" where they were locked and gassed. Those soldiers who died without a comforting word strewn on battlefields. Or the clear message of a military cemetery. I often had the chance to visit the American cemetery at Nettuno in Italy on the Mediterranean coast, not far from Anzio where the landing of troops in World War II took place. There are endless rows of crosses and stars of David in perfect symmetry, against the background of well-kept green grass. The scene never failed to move me. One has to meditate on those lives snuffed out by a sole factor, the arrogance of power. These were young people who never had the chance to marry or look into the eyes of their first child, to finish college and launch a career, to grow old surrounded by love, and to exit this world leaving a posterity of children and grandchildren. Death considered by itself alone is indeed "the Grim Reaper." When it strikes the young or arrives in tragic ways, it is truly numbing. What is to be learned from these great lessons in life? They require reflection, and the lesson may often be a negative one. So be it. In speaking to us of fragility, power-lessness, and total brokenness, death is still a window on God.

HOW LONG, LORD?

Yet there must be a bright horizon beyond all of this. The God of Israel is a God of hope; the God of Jesus is the promise of immortality. It is with the breaking of the fifth seal that the first semblance of dawn appears. As the holy dead cry out from their altar grave, they echo our own sentiments: "How long, O Lord, how long?" Is human suffering to be endless? When will God be vindicated? How many times in life people indicate that they have reached their limits. Perhaps we can all be counted among their number. We can go no further; the breaking point has been reached. But then we have the courage to move ahead a bit.

Suffering is endurable because faith tells us that there is a future. And hope builds on faith. As Christians, this hope is rooted in our present life in Christ. Our life in the Spirit is the door to immortal-ity. We are convinced that there must be an end to our anguished cry. And there is always the reality of the suffering God. What we endure, especially in the cause of Christ, is "fellowship in his suffer-ings." In the mystery of the one Body, our sufferings become part of his, just as our victory will be a share in his (Phil 3:9f). And so we too cry out from the base of the altar: "When will our experience of evil be ended, Lord? When will your kingdom of peace and love be fully established? Come, Lord Jesus!" We live in hope.

EARTHQUAKE

The sixth seal ushers in the final cataclysm, a veritable *Götterdämmerung*, the final moments of Wagner's monumental

Ring Cycle when Valhalla, the castle of the gods, crumbles in total devastation. With the stars plummeting and the moon blood red, the earth is rocked by frightful quakes. Earthquakes have become all too frequent visitors to our planet in recent years. What is terrifying about them is the realization that there is nothing one can do. For the most part one is utterly trapped; there is no warning, and their duration is all too brief.

The earthquake that struck central Italy in 1997 was not the most devastating but was among the most poignant. When it struck the city of Assisi, it meant loss and homelessness for many people of the region. In destroying a part of the basilica of St. Francis and its priceless art, as well as taking the lives of friars and citizens, it reached the town's most celebrated and beloved citizen. A certain sadness reached the world at large, for this is a bigger-than-life saint who belongs to the world. In the Assisi earthquake, the sacred and the profane were brought into startling juxtaposition. The sacred, the beautiful, the saintly were profoundly struck by the unleashed forces of an unpredictable nature. Assisi represents much that is the best in us, but it now speaks as well of a creation, itself tainted by sin, which can speak in ungodly terms. And yet with it all, as scripture states, creation itself is redeemed by the blood of the Lamb. And just as certainly as Assisi will rise like the phoenix from its own ashes, so the days of the Dragon, in Revelation's terms, are limited. The fall of Valhalla was followed by the bright dawning of a new day. It reflects our faith. And on this we stand.

The Question of Evil

1. The Bible posits a connection between moral evil and cosmic evil. What is our understanding of that link?

2. In what way can you see a war as being justified today?

3. How do you think our modern age looks at death?

4. Famine is hard to accept in this world of such abundant food. Is there a viable solution to the problem?

5. How do you continue to hope in the midst of great tragedy?

THE SIGNING OF THE ELECT (7:1–17)

7:1 After this I saw four angels standing at the four corners of the earth, holding back the four winds of the earth so that no wind could blow on land or sea or against any tree.

7:2 Then I saw another angel come up from the East, holding the seal of the living God. He cried out in a loud voice to the four angels who were given power to damage the land and the sea,

7:3 "Do not damage the land or the sea or the trees until we put the seal on the foreheads of the servants of our God."

7:4 I heard the number of those who had been marked with the seal, one hundred and forty-four thousand marked from every tribe of the Israelites:

7:5 twelve thousand were marked from the tribe of Judah, twelve thousand from the tribe of Reuben, twelve thousand from the tribe of Gad,

7:6 twelve thousand from the tribe of Asher, twelve thousand from the tribe of Naphtali, twelve thousand from the tribe of Manasseh,

7:7 twelve thousand from the tribe of Simeon, twelve thousand from the tribe of Levi, twelve thousand from the tribe of Issachar,

7:8 twelve thousand from the tribe of Zebulun, twelve thousand from the tribe of Joseph, and twelve thousand were marked from the tribe of Benjamin.

7:9 After this I had a vision of a great multitude, which no one could count, from every nation, race, people, and tongue. They stood before the throne and before the Lamb, wearing white robes and holding palm branches in their hands.

7:10 They cried out in a loud voice:
"Salvation comes from our God, who is seated on the throne,
 and from the Lamb."

7:11 All the angels stood around the throne and around the elders and the four living creatures. They prostrated themselves before the throne, worshiped God,

7:12 and exclaimed:
"Amen. Blessing and glory, wisdom and thanksgiving,
honor, power, and might
be to our God forever and ever. Amen."

7:13 Then one of the elders spoke up and said to me, "Who are these wearing white robes, and where did they come from?"

7:14 I said to him, "My lord, you are the one who knows." He said to me, "These are the ones who have survived the time of great distress; they have washed their robes and made them white in the blood of the Lamb.

7:15 "For this reason they stand before God's throne
and worship him day and night in his temple.
The one who sits on the throne will shelter them.

7:16 They will not hunger or thirst anymore,
nor will the sun or any heat strike them.

7:17 For the Lamb who is in the center of the throne will
  shepherd them
  and lead them to springs of life-giving water,
  and God will wipe away every tear from their eyes."

There is an interruption in the picture of destruction with this positive addition on the salvation of the elect. It is presented in two scenes, one earthly (vv. 1–8) and one heavenly (vv. 9–17). Four angels *(v. 1): They stand at the four corners of the earth and temporarily stay all the winds and evils of the six seals.* The seal on the forehead *(v. 3) (Gr.: sphragizo): The symbol of baptismal incorporation (2 Cor 1:22; Eph 1:13; 4:30). There is a call for the cessation of all calamity until the saved are sealed.*

The number of the elect is clearly symbolic of a great multitude. It is the twelve tribes of Israel times the twelve apostles, again multiplied by one thousand (12 x 12 x 1,000). These are the elect within the Judeo-Christian tradition, the fulfillment of Israel, the full complement of the church. The multiplication of the symbolic twelve and twelve by a thousand simply makes it incredibly large, an "astronomical" number.

The next presentation is that of the church in glory (vv. 9–17). This

is not another group but rather a transposition to a new key, as the elect are now viewed in terms of their universal character (v. 9). White robes and palm branches *(v. 9): Signs of baptismal holiness, joy, and victory (6:11; Col 3:8–10; 1 Mc 13:51).*

The first hymn *(v. 10), a song of the redeemed, gives recognition for salvation to both God and Christ.*

The second hymn *(v. 12) is voiced by angels, the elders, and the four living creatures.* Amen *(v. 12): This is a response to the former hymn (v. 10). The attributes are seven, all previously mentioned (5:12–13). They combine personal qualities (wisdom, power, might) with attributions from outside (blessing, honor, glory, thanksgiving). The hymn here is sung to God alone, the source of all salvation.*

The elect are pictured here as having already endured the great duress. They have experienced the fruits of Christ's saving death and are presented as passing through any end-time desolation. Here we must avoid trying to establish a temporal sequence from one scene to another of the book. Rather it is a kaleidoscopic picture of final salvation, which revolves around different points of emphasis.

The third hymn *(vv. 15–17) is idyllic and draws on a number of biblical images. With final victory attained, God is the center of endless worship, a joy stripped of every vestige of misfortune.* No hunger or thirst *(v. 16): Isaiah 49:10.* The Lamb will shepherd them *(v. 17): Psalm 23; 1 Peter 2:25, 5:4; Matthew 9:36.* Wipe away every tear *(v. 17): Isaiah 25:8. The contrast between the woes of the six seals and the picture of deliverance in this chapter makes an exciting contrast. The different hues, overlays, and atemporal scenarios is true apocalyptic, as heaven and earth are joined in this end-time vision.*

FULFILLMENT AND INCLUSION

The somber picture connected with the six seals is interrupted by a scene of brilliant contrast. It is the moment of victory, the salvation of God's elect. There is no question of establishing some sort of sequence here. We are faced with a striking literary expression of colors of varying and contrasting hues, juxtaposing light and darkness. The imagery envelops us with its demands to be accepted on its own terms without having predetermined logical forms imposed upon it.

The 144,000 people sealed and saved draw us immediately to the history of salvation. The twelve tribes of Israel blend with the twelve apostles to give us a sense of tradition and fulfillment. The square of twelve multiplied by one thousand brings to full complement the history of salvation. Israel becomes church. Church becomes all-inclusive. This chapter of Revelation roots us in tradition and at the same time stretches our vision to a point of universal inclusiveness. There is an inherent complementarity in this vision, but there are tensions as well. As Catholics we are caught up in a tradition that spans centuries. It includes our Hebrew roots as well as our creeds, councils, liturgical forms, and moral behavior, and in a special way, our theologies. It cherishes a literature that moves from the Church Fathers through the Middle Ages, the Renaissance, and the Enlightenment into modern times. Art and music gave expression to belief in every age and form part of the Christian patrimony.

There have been moments of great change in this tradition. When God was the supreme center of life, we had sweeping Gothic cathedrals, Gregorian chant, and polyphony, all of which pointed to the otherness of the deity. This history saw the incorporation of Plato and Aristotle into a language about the Judeo-Christian God, and a hierarchy that began with God and worked in descending steps toward the faithful. With the Renaissance and, more strikingly, the Enlightenment, the human person became the norm of everything, and the distinction between the profane and sacred became blurred. Art found as much in mythology as in religious history and centered on the human form. There was now music for the salon and the theater, not solely for church and cloister. In literature there was concern for the human psyche and its aspirations. In theology new questions were raised in attempts to interpret a changing reality. There were fewer pat answers, less black and white, more grays.

THE PATRIMONY

Today change seems endless. It has become a way of life. Paradigm shifts have become a matter of course. It is in moments such as this, a time of great flux, that an appreciation of tradition takes on special importance. Our new insights build on an incredibly long patrimony. Once that link is lost, we are very much at sea. When our courses in theology do not interface with the past, then we are bound to create an atmosphere of insecurity with little appreciation for the ground on which we stand. If our seminary students in the years immediately following Vatican II were excited about new conciliar directions, it was because they had been schooled in the tradition and could better cope with new insights. In those days one rarely encountered a conservative reaction in the classroom. In the 1990s it was quite a different story, when a sharp move to the right among students was much more in evidence. The reasons for this are not easily reduced to one simple answer. At least in part, we transitioned too quickly and often neglected our past as we moved ahead in the post-conciliar years. Inferior catechetics and a generally vague understanding of what our basic beliefs are wreaked considerable damage on an entire generation of young people. People grew into adulthood walking on the shifting sands of uncertainty and became in time quite reactionary in the face of new directions. This explains at least in part how it can happen that two generations interface and fail to understand each other. An earlier generation, better rooted in the tradition, welcomed solid new directions and insights that scholarship made possible. A new generation looks for the anchor in the face of what appears to be a very relative approach to religious truth.

While this retrenching can become a very frustrating experience, it does point up the importance of the patrimony and of seeing growth as a logical progression from one step to another. It is lamentable that Latin and the biblical languages are given little more than a passing nod today as people prepare for church ministries, especially priesthood. Only in recent times has there been a revival of the great musical tradition of the church, with the recognition that active participation in liturgy does not exclude the role of the choir in the use of classical polyphony as well as contemporary music or plain chant for the congregation. Our tradition embraces the breadth of Christian culture, developed over many centuries. As the symbolic elect of Revelation find themselves rooted in the ancient prophets and sages, as well as the later apostles, we too must never forget our past.

APPRECIATING THE NEW

But Revelation also looks at the new. There stood before God and the Lamb a great multitude from every race, nation, people, and tongue. This is not a Palestinian Jewish-Christian culture, still enamored of the Law and its trappings. Quite the opposite. This is a new era marked by inclusiveness. The same is true of the church today. We are not simply a prolongation of the past, the champions of the achieved position. Just as Jesus was a startling innovator with radical demands who alienated many of his contemporaries, so too the church at a very early period had to decide how it would adjust to the new demands placed upon it. What was to become of the Jewish law and ritual? Would circumcision continue to be binding? It was a moment of truth in deciding whether Christianity would be simply another sect of Judaism or an all-inclusive religion. And this sense of innovation has been with the church over the centuries. As it became increasingly a religion of every race and nation, Christianity had to establish clearly its nonnegotiables in faith while drawing on the new cultures that it encountered. Today the situation is no different; it is just that demands are more numerous and come at a faster pace. The advances in biblical scholarship in the twentieth century have been truly incredible. Serious scholarship has been able to separate chaff from wheat in making the biblical text more comprehensible. Theological development, very closely related to the biblical renewal, has carried human reflection on Revelation to important new plateaus. Liturgy has assumed once again its rightful place as the apogee of the Christian life. In these and other areas we have experienced immense change over the past fifty years; many of us are grateful and deeply chagrined by the "voices of doom" that see the council and its aftermath in largely negative terms. And there is no reason to think that change will stop. We are not members of a static church but rather are a people of God that continues to wend its way through history.

INTEGRATION

The lesson to be learned from the "double vision" of chapter 7 is the importance of integration. Polarization arises from an inability or an unwillingness to bring the past and the present together. Alexander Pope wisely suggested that we "be not the first by whom the new is tried, nor the last to lay the old aside." If all good theology is pastoral, then it is capable of integrating the achieved position and the new direction. Today the task is formidable indeed, but it remains indispensable. And we must be of good heart. The present moment is not the end. We have succeeded in centuries past; there is every reason to believe that we shall do so again.

The Meaning of Salvation

1. What is the role of the Lamb with the six seals?

2. Nature can be seen as either a friend or foe of humanity. Cite some examples of each.

3. Natural disasters usually take the greatest toll on the poorest people. How can we see that in terms of God's plan?

4. Explain the significance of the white garment placed on the child in baptism.

5. "I want to be saved." How do you understand that expression?

6. The church in Revelation is seen as the new Israel. How do you understand that designation?

7. The church is universal. What are the practical implications of that belief?

8. How do we accept change in the church and still cherish the patrimony?

THE FIRST SIX TRUMPETS (8:1–9:21)

8:1 **When he broke open the seventh seal, there was silence in heaven for about half an hour.**

8:2 **And I saw that the seven angels who stood before God were given seven trumpets.**

THE GOLD CENSER

8:3 Another angel came and stood at the altar, holding a gold censer. He was given a great quantity of incense to offer, along with the prayers of all the holy ones, on the gold altar that was before the throne.

8:4 The smoke of the incense along with the prayers of the holy ones went up before God from the hand of the angel.

8:5 Then the angel took the censer, filled it with burning coals from the altar, and hurled it down to the earth. There were peals of thunder, rumblings, flashes of lightning, and an earthquake.

THE FIRST FOUR TRUMPETS

8:6 The seven angels who were holding the seven trumpets prepared to blow them.

8:7 When the first one blew his trumpet, there came hail and fire mixed with blood, which was hurled down to the earth. A third of the land was burned up, along with a third of the trees and all green grass.

8:8 When the second angel blew his trumpet, something like a large burning mountain was hurled into the sea. A third of the sea turned to blood,

8:9 a third of the creatures living in the sea died, and a third of the ships were wrecked.

8:10 When the third angel blew his trumpet, a large star burning like a torch fell from the sky. It fell on a third of the rivers and on the springs of water.

8:11 The star was called "Wormwood," and a third of all the water turned to wormwood. Many people died from this water, because it was made bitter.

8:12 When the fourth angel blew his trumpet, a third of the sun, a third of the moon, and a third of the stars were struck, so that a third of them became dark. The day lost its light for a third of the time, as did the night.

8:13 Then I looked again and heard an eagle flying high overhead cry out in a loud voice, "Woe! Woe! Woe to the inhabitants of the earth from the rest of the trumpet blasts that the three angels are about to blow!"

THE FIFTH TRUMPET

9:1 Then the fifth angel blew his trumpet, and I saw a star that had fallen from the sky to the earth. It was given the key for the passage to the abyss.

9:2 It opened the passage to the abyss, and smoke came up out of the passage like smoke from a huge furnace. The sun and the air were darkened by the smoke from the passage.

9:3 Locusts came out of the smoke onto the land, and they were given the same power as scorpions of the earth.

9:4 They were told not to harm the grass of the earth or any plant or any tree, but only those people who did not have the seal of God on their foreheads.

9:5 They were not allowed to kill them but only to torment them for five months; the torment they inflicted was like that of a scorpion when it stings a person.

9:6 During that time these people will seek death but will not find it, and they will long to die but death will escape them.

9:7 The appearance of the locusts was like that of horses ready for battle. On their heads they wore what looked like crowns of gold; their faces were like human faces,

9:8 and they had hair like women's hair. Their teeth were like lions' teeth,

9:9 and they had chests like iron breastplates. The sound of their wings was like the sound of many horse-drawn chariots racing into battle.

9:10 They had tails like scorpions, with stingers; with their tails they had power to harm people for five months.

9:11 They had as their king the angel of the abyss, whose name in Hebrew is Abaddon and in Greek Apollyon.

9:12 The first woe has passed, but there are two more to come.

THE SIXTH TRUMPET

9:13 Then the sixth angel blew his trumpet, and I heard a voice coming from the [four] horns of the gold altar before God,

9:14 telling the sixth angel who held the trumpet, "Release the four angels who are bound at the banks of the great river Euphrates."

9:15 So the four angels were released, who were prepared for this hour, day, month, and year to kill a third of the human race.

9:16 The number of cavalry troops was two hundred million; I heard their number.

9:17 Now in my vision this is how I saw the horses and their riders. They wore red, blue, and yellow breastplates, and the horses' heads were like heads of lions, and out of their mouths came fire, smoke, and sulfur.

9:18 By these three plagues of fire, smoke, and sulfur that came out of their mouths a third of the human race was killed.

9:19 For the power of the horses is in their mouths and in their tails; for their tails are like snakes, with heads that inflict harm.

9:20 The rest of the human race, who were not killed by these plagues, did not repent of the works of their hands, to give up the worship of demons and idols made from gold, silver, bronze, stone, and wood, which cannot see or hear or walk.

9:21 Nor did they repent of their murders, their magic potions, their unchastity, or their robberies.

The opening of the seventh seal *(8:1–5) is prelude to the next set of woes to be ushered in by the trumpet blasts. This is preceded by one-half hour of silence (v. 1), which may refer to Zephaniah's silence before the Day of the Lord (Zep 1:7). Late Jewish literature also spoke of the silence before the work of God in the initial creation (4 Ezr 10:2). The prayer of the elect for deliverance is described in the metaphor of smoke from the burning incense, rising in God's presence (vv. 3–4; Ps 141:2). The prayer and incense blend together in the mediation of the ministering angel.*

As the prayer of incense quickly turns into the censer of burning coals

of destruction hurled to the earth, the faithful ones are evidently onlookers and not victims. The ensuing cataclysm is then prelude to the woes of the trumpets. Trumpets were part of liturgy (2 Chr 5:12–13), theophany (Ex 19:16), and eschatological announcement (Is 27:13; Mt 24:31). The imagery that is used in describing each of the trumpet woes, as will be seen later in the case of the bowls, draws heavily on the Exodus plagues (Ex 7–11).

The First Four Trumpets (vv. 6–13)

The afflictions consist of:

   • *A torrential downpour of blood, hail, and fire. Recalls the hail and lightning of the seventh plague (Ex 9:22–25).*

   • *A burning mountain hits the blood-drenched sea. Recalls the bloody waters of the first plague (Ex 7:20).*

   • *A burning star hits the rivers.*

   • *Darkness ensues from loss of part of the sea, the moon, and the stars. Recalls the ninth plague of darkness in Egypt (Ex 10:12).*

It is again important to note the absence of any real chronology. The images are not sequential but are best read as a continual surrealistic overlay. Thus the grass may be burned at one moment (8:7) but is still present in another (9:41). The stars are hit (8:12) but have already fallen (6:13). In addition, there are repeated allusions to the plagues of Egypt; they are here given a cosmic dimension. The land, sea, rivers, and stars are all affected as history comes to a close.

Wormwood (v. 11) (Gr.: apsinthos): A bitter plant used symbolically to depict an infliction of suffering and death (Dt 29:17; Jer 9:14; 23:15).

Just as the half-hour silence served as a dramatic prelude to the trumpet woes, so too the soaring eagle with its plaintive cry (v. 13) leads into the sorrowful moments to follow (9:12; 11:14). The fifth and sixth trumpets will herald tragic news; the seventh and final, however, sets another tone. Like the seventh seal, at its opening (8:1–4) it will be marked by heavenly peace and joy.

The Fifth and Sixth Trumpets (c. 9)

These are the two climactic woes: an invasion of demonic locusts (vv. 1–12) and one of horses (vv. 13–20). A star (v. 1): Although fallen powers are often depicted as stars (Is 14:12–15), the reference here is symbolic of an angel (1:20; 20:1); it carries the key to the lower realm. The abyss *(v. 2): Sheol, the underworld, the realm of the dead. It is depicted as being connected with the earth by a long passageway with a covering at the top, opened by the angel-star. Smoke pours out of the passage.*

The emerging locusts immediately suggest the eighth Egyptian plague (vv. 3ff; Ex 10:12–15), here placed in an eschatological setting to match Joel's army of locusts (Jl 1–2) and equipped with the scorpion's sting (v. 5; Ez 2:6). Unlike the former plagues, the locusts bring no harm upon the land but only attack people (the evildoers), and even then, they torment them but do not kill them (v. 6). The description of the locusts is surrealistic and highly mythological (vv. 7–11). We can, however, identify the source of most of the imagery: war horses *(Jl 2:4),* lions' teeth *(Jl 1:6),* wings of chariot noise *(Jl 2:5). Additional features include the human faces, women's hair, and the crowned heads.*

The angel or messenger leading the invading horde is called Abaddon, *which in Hebrew means "destruction," and in its Greek form* Apollyon *is personalized, that is, the destroyer. Although leading a menacing force, Abaddon remains a legate of God, even though this imagery contributed to the popular idea of Satan as a fallen angel (Lk 10:18). It is hard to determine any specific significance in the five-month duration of the attack (v. 10), other than to recognize the imposed limits on the punishment.*

The sixth trumpet heralds the arrival of the army of horses, which has an equally strange composition (vv. 13–21). The source of this invasion comes from the heavenly altar; an unidentified voice gives the command to the sixth angel with the trumpet (v. 13). The order is to release four menacing angels who have been restrained at the Euphrates, and they in turn introduce the plague of the horses (v. 14). The mystery is maintained by the absence of any causal connection in the sequence.

The reference to the Euphrates again suggests the Roman enemy, the Parthians, who were located beyond the great river, but here the enemy is raised to apocalyptic status. The limitation on punishment remains very clear both as to time (v. 15) and extent of damage (v. 18). The four angels seem to be at the head of the invading force, although such is not specifically indicated. The size of the army is intentionally "beyond imagination" in its number of two hundred million. Signs of torture surround the appearance of the horses and riders: the colors of the breastplates (red, blue, and yellow) match the fire, smoke, and sulfur emissions of the horses (vv. 17f). The horses' mouths spew destruction, and their serpent tails bite their opponents. With its clashing imagery, the picture is jarring indeed!

With it all, after six terrifying plagues, the living onlookers still do not repent (vv. 20f). In a literary sense, they cannot repent because the dreaded Day is not yet at an end. The sins of which they are guilty are decalogue-related, with a special accent on idolatry. Delving into magic seems to have been one of the signs of the times (Acts 19:18–19). This scene brings to a conclusion the period of the six trumpets, which followed the seven seals.

SILENCE AND PRAYER

The opening of the seventh seal is not an endpoint; it inaugurates a new series of disasters related to the seven trumpets. In this unusual unfolding of the end time, we seem to be led down endless corridors as one series of disasters leads into another. But we are given occasional moments of respite, which are thrown into welcome relief when viewed against the somber background of "gloom and doom." As the seventh seal is opened, and before the blast of the first trumpet, there is a very significant pause, a silence that lasts thirty minutes. This serves to build the dramatic tension as the narrative continues to unfold. It is in its setting an eerie silence with a certain foreboding character. But it is followed at once by the prayers of the church, the holy ones, the elect, with the captivating image of prayer ascending to God like incense from a burning censer. The contrast continues as the censer, a symbol of adoration and homage, becomes an instrument of destruction as it is hurled to the earth. The moment of peace and reverie has passed.

There are musical pauses that enhance the beauty of a symphony or concerto. We catch our breath and remain poised for the next outpouring of melody. There are pauses in drama when silence can carry the plot forward more than a thousand words. Even in comedy the pause has its place. Those old enough to remember the radio comedian Jack Benny are able to recall how he capitalized on the "silent response" and elicited great laughter.

CONTEMPLATION

Silence can enunciate many things in life, some of them positive, some negative. There is a timeless truth that says that our spiritual life cannot grow without silence. It explains the contemplative life in the church and the emphasis silence receives in all the spiritual masters. It is not hard to find people who are very uncomfortable with silence and tend to shun solitude. They are trapped in a world of continuous sound and are uneasy when it ceases. Yet, to commune with God and to get to know him, a certain space has to be provided. The mind must be at rest and capable of focusing on the center of our life. Meditation can no more be discarded than it can be forced. And many of us can remember when meditation, like everything else in our life, was compartmentalized, and we experienced difficulty in getting our racing minds and imaginations to settle down and to get off the heavily traveled freeway.

We know that silence is found for different people in different places. A quiet chapel, a verdant hillside, the quiet of one's own room. The early morning, the break at mid-day, the late hours of the night. For some people the hustle and bustle of a busy airport can be a place of intense prayer. What is important is that one can stand before the Lord or before the Lamb and center solely on the God of love. It is quite true that we can find God in our work, our community, and in our leisure. But for this there must be an interplay with the time of solitude. And the encouraging note is that the more we engage in silence the more we grow to love it. God draws ever closer to us in tenderness, in forgiveness, in mercy. And when silence is truly understood, we never really feel alone. And that is because we never really are. In those moments, the God of the covenant who is the God of love draws very close to us. What goes into that time or how it is best used is a personal matter and rests with the individual. But to say that we do not have the time is to be lost in activity, with little or nothing left on reserve when the trying moments come. "In heaven there was silence for about half an hour."

SPEAKING TO GOD...

"Let my prayer come like incense before you, Lord." How many times have we watched the wafting smoke from a burning censer ascend, often passing through rays of sunlight refracted through stained glass windows. And even if the biblical metaphor had not come to the fore long before us, it would certainly remind us of our prayer. We pray because in faith we believe that our prayers do rise to God. It is our response in covenant love expressed in allegiance, devotion, and utter dependence. And it is a loving conversation. Saint Irenaeus says that in praying we speak to God, and in reading the divine oracles God speaks to us. What does God ask of me? When does he do the talking? When does the incense smoke come drifting back to earth? *Tolle et lege.* "Take and read." To draw on the scriptures is to hear God speak. To nurture that Word, to integrate it, to move it to the center of my life is to pray. To be Christian means to bear Christ's name, to be in a true relationship with him, and to see the world through his eyes. In Revelation it is the elect, the faithful ones who are at prayer. Those destined for doom are simply disconnected; prayer has no part in their life.

A visit to Lourdes was, for me, a powerful experience of prayer. My first visit there was in the late 1950s. The two most powerful images that remain with me to this day are silence and prayer. From the moment I passed through the grotto gates, the silence was all-pervasive. It was a silence that thundered: "This is holy ground." And the sense of prayer! It was the height of summer marked by the presence of thousands of pilgrims. There were the wheel-chaired infirm and the many young university students who had volunteered to assist them. Many of the sick returned year after year, always hoping for a cure but always leaving with a renewed faith. The message they sent to me and to many others was one of fidelity, cheerfulness, and patience. Even with faith we know it is hard to make sense of life. The questions are as old as those posed by Job and Ecclesiastes. But the believer holds on, fully realizing that God is not capricious or unfeeling. He is at all cost the loving God who has spoken irrevocably in Jesus. Prayer brings that truth to life in the face of the most enigmatic situations.

Silence and prayer come together in unexpected ways as well. There is a silence that seeks to exclude. We all know what it is to receive the "silent treatment." Someone no longer wishes to communicate with us, and therefore we are ignored. This is an unwelcome type of silence and can cause considerable pain. This is the use of silence as a weapon. The Word urges us to overcome and eliminate such hostility in "not letting the sun go down on our anger," even if we are not the guilty party. And it is precisely here that prayer can prove to be a peaceful ally. We bring the other person before the Lord and pray for the grace to overcome. Love is always more powerful than hate; the Gospels make that eminently clear. And even when the best results are not forthcoming, perseverance brings a certain peace in knowing that our personal intentions are the best.

This part of Revelation presents a powerful pause before the trumpets bring fire, blood, and locusts. Lack of repentance spells doom; not even God can overcome hardness of heart. But the "escape clause" is always there. Turn to the Lord and be saved. The elect know it all too well. In the face of disaster, their voices rise to God like burning incense.

In Terms of My Own Life...

1. Do I feel the need for more silence in my life?

2. Do I have sufficient time for prayer? Do I cherish that time?

3. How do I relate prayer and action?

4. How do I deal with silent hostility?

5. Tradition sees a strong relationship between silence and prayer. Do I share that belief?

PROPHETIC WITNESS AND THE SEVENTH TRUMPET (10:1–11:19)

THE ANGEL WITH THE SMALL SCROLL

10:1 Then I saw another mighty angel come down from heaven wrapped in a cloud, with a halo around his head; his face was like the sun and his feet were like pillars of fire.

10:2 In his hand he held a small scroll that had been opened. He placed his right foot on the sea and his left foot on the land,

10:3 and then he cried out in a loud voice as a lion roars. When he cried out, the seven thunders raised their voices, too.

10:4 When the seven thunders had spoken, I was about to write it down; but I heard a voice from heaven say, "Seal up what the seven thunders have spoken, but do not write it down."

10:5 Then the angel I saw standing on the sea and on the land raised his right hand to heaven

10:6 and swore by the one who lives forever and ever, who created heaven and earth and sea and all that is in them, "There shall be no more delay.

10:7 At the time when you hear the seventh angel blow his trumpet, the mysterious plan of God shall be fulfilled, as he promised to his servants the prophets."

10:8 Then the voice that I had heard from heaven spoke to me again and said, "Go, take the scroll that lies open in the hand of the angel who is standing on the sea and on the land."

10:9 So I went up to the angel and told him to give me the small scroll. He said to me, "Take and swallow it. It will turn your stomach sour, but in your mouth it will taste as sweet as honey."

10:10 I took the small scroll from the angel's hand and swallowed it. In my mouth it was like sweet honey, but when I had eaten it, my stomach turned sour.

10:11 Then someone said to me, "You must prophesy again about many peoples, nations, tongues, and kings."

There are two scenes that anticipate the final trumpet blast (11:15): the angel with the scroll (c. 10) and the two witnesses (11:1–13). Two Old Testament texts are operative in chapter 10: Psalms 29:3–9 and Ezekiel 3:1–3.

In chapter 10, the angel has all the characteristics of Yahweh: wrapped in a cloud *(v. 1; Ex 16:10; 1 Kgs 8:10);* halo around his head *(v. 1; 4:3);* face like the sun *(v. 1; 1:16);* feet like pillars of fire *(v. 1; 1:15).* Voice like thunder *(v. 3): This symbol of majesty and power is evocative of Psalms 29:3–9; even the number seven appears in both. The message itself is not delineated (v. 4). It is heard but not to be written, so it is "sealed" only figuratively. The brevity of time before the end may account for its not being written down.*

The angel's posture, resembling the legendary Colossus, spans sea and land and thus symbolizes a universal reign (vv. 5–6). The proximity of judgment directly echoes the same dictum in Daniel (12:7). And it will be wholly in accord with what has been predicted (v. 6): "There shall be no more delay."

The figure of John the seer is present throughout the chapter. The scroll in the angel's hand (v. 2) comes into play at the chapter's end (vv. 9–10). He is told to eat the scroll, in a scene echoing Ezekiel (3:1–13). As the Word of God, it has the sweetness of divine communication and the promise of a positive outcome, but, as a message of suffering and destruction, it is sour as well.

SWEET AND SOUR

Both the seer of Patmos and Ezekiel were told to eat the Word of God and for both it was sweet-tasting in the mouth. But for John, the visionary, it turned sour in the stomach. In Revelation it is a question of good news and bad news. The bad news, connected with the dyspeptic stomach, spelled destruction and devastation, which is so much in evidence in the book itself. But ultimately there will be good news as well: the final victory of God's elect. Are there shades of our own story in all of this that are worth bearing in mind?

To know the scriptures and to attempt to live them brings an immense consolation. As we repeatedly ask ourselves, "What does God ask of me?" it is in reading the scriptures that the answer emerges. Our understanding of God, his engagement in human history, the sending of his Son, deliverance from sin, and the true message of hope are all to be found in a prayerful reading of the Word of God. Our moral conduct is addressed in Paul's letters, the Gospel of John, the sermon on the mount, and the many parables of the synoptic gospels. A former student of mine, who had long endured the harshness of an unloving father, grew up projecting the same characteristics on God. A deep sense of guilt for sin, the assurance of punishment, and the fear of final separation and damnation were dominant features of his life. At a relatively early age, however, he became interested in the Gospel of Luke and began to read it intently. The image of a loving and forgiving God, so central to the Lucan presentation of Jesus, gave this young man a totally different understanding of God and set his life on a whole new track. By the time I taught him he was a seminary student well on his way to a life of ministry in the church. The scroll had become sweet in his mouth.

The story of the incarnation itself lifts our spirit; the death and rising of Jesus reaches us personally in the paschal mystery. We are people of hope and courage for whom there is always a happy outcome. Or to paraphrase Paul, if God has loved us this far, do you think he is going to give up on us now? Inner peace does not mean some sort of euphoria or a passing "glow"; rather it is deep and real and as permanent as faith itself. We have all encountered this in life. There are those people whose serenity is constant, those for whom the present tragedy is never the last word, those who find in God's Word a consolation that is inestimable.

THE LIFE-GIVING SCRIPTURES

Tolle et lege. "Take and read." The scriptures should be our daily bread. As much as other important authors, past or present, may engage us, they can never have the significance of God's own Word. The age when Catholics were not encouraged to read the Bible is still a living memory. Even in seminary life, books for meditation and spiritual reading were drawn from the great masters of the ascetical life. But the scriptures were read rather sparingly and then only in a translation from the Latin version, not from the original Hebrew and Greek. All of that, of course, is now in the past, and we are encouraged to turn to that most precious source of life. The more we do so, the sweeter the taste as we savor its message, a message that is meant to be translated into life. If we have been the cause of pain to another, the gospel is clear on what we must do. If others have injured us and we feel wounded, forgiveness becomes the order of the day. If someone needs us, even if our time is precious and our resources limited, then let that person have "the tunic and the cloak as well." This is not to say that the New Testament answers every ethical problem that occurs in modern life. But in painting with broad strokes, it sets forth the principles and offers a program of action that moves us toward application.

THE PAIN OF THE WORD

But the seer discovered that what was sweet in the mouth could give him indigestion as well. Would that it were all sweetness and light! The fact is that God's Word makes strong demands and moves us away from the plateau of the "status quo." Is it not true that the major reforms in Christianity were biblically rooted? One may agree or disagree with the sixteenth-century reformers and qualify their positions in various ways, but there is no denying the fact that they were scripturally rooted. There was always the feeling that the farther church life drifted from its biblical moorings, the greater the danger of infidelity. It was the gospel life that was pursued and with no small amount of pain.

Biblical faith is not simply a private and personal adherence to the Lord. It also has ecclesial and social consequences. And once it moves from the privacy of our room and into the street and the marketplace, the pain begins. We see today so many examples of the cost of gospel conviction. The civil rights movement was founded on religious principles, in defense of which some paid with their lives. Then there has been the ongoing opposition to abortion; it too has been a painful struggle, as is true as well in the case of assisted suicide. In upholding the sacredness of human life, both have strong biblical roots. By early 1998, 437 persons had been executed in the United States since the restoration of the death penalty. How can Christians find this tolerable in the light of Christ's call to forgiveness, pardon, and the elimination of any hostile feelings? And yet opposition to any or all of these assaults on human life results in hardship, rejection, and discouragement. Vocal opposition is certainly part of the American tradition, but that does not make it easier. This is scripture making its demands and taking its toll. But if faith does not lead to this, then it is a very anemic type of faith.

It is unfortunate that a stand on principle is often viewed with hostility. But there again the principled Christian cannot return hatred with hatred or with any form of animosity. We can never be negative people. The scroll may often taste bitter but it is also sweet, and it is precisely that sweetness, even in the defense of principle, which must be evident in our comportment.

As long as we live in the meantime, caught between the "now" and the "not yet," we are living in tension. We are caught in the crossfire for simply doing what we believe is right. And yet we return to the theme with which we began. A life lived in biblical faith is coherent, consoling, and life-giving. The dyspeptic stomach is not the final word. The assurance of good health with the sweet savor of the scroll restored is a deep-rooted biblical conviction. Evil may have its day, but good will triumph.

THE TWO WITNESSES

11:1 **Then I was given a measuring rod like a staff and I was told, "Come and measure the temple of God and the altar. Count those who are worshipping in it.**

11:2 **But exclude the outer court of the temple, do not measure it, for it has been handed over to the Gentiles, who will trample the holy city for forty-two months.**

11:3 **I will commission my two witnesses to prophesy for those twelve hundred and sixty days, wearing sackcloth."**

11:4 **These are the two olive trees and the two lampstands that stand before the Lord of the earth.**

11:5 **If anyone wants to harm them, fire comes out of their** mouths and devours their enemies. In this way, anyone wanting to harm them is sure to be slain.

11:6 They have the power to close up the sky so that no rain can fall during the time of their prophesying. They also have power to turn water into blood and to afflict the earth with any plague as often as they wish.

11:7 When they have finished their testimony, the beast that comes up from the abyss will wage war against them and conquer them and kill them.

11:8 Their corpses will lie in the main street of the great city, which has the symbolic name "Sodom" and "Egypt," where indeed the Lord was crucified.

11:9 Those from every people, tribe, tongue, and nation will gaze on their corpses for three and a half days, and they will not allow their corpses to be buried.

11:10 The inhabitants of the earth will gloat over them and be glad and exchange gifts because these two prophets tormented the inhabitants of the earth.

11:11 But after three and a half days, a breath of life from God entered them. When they stood on their feet, great fear fell on those who saw them.

11:12 Then they heard a loud voice from heaven say to them, "Come up here." So they went up to heaven in a cloud as their enemies looked on.

11:13 At that moment there was a great earthquake, and a tenth of the city fell in ruins. Seven thousand people were killed during the earthquake; the rest were terrified and gave glory to the God of heaven.

11:14 The second woe has passed, but the third is coming soon.

THE SEVENTH TRUMPET

11:15 Then the seventh angel blew his trumpet. There were loud voices in heaven, saying, "The kingdom of the world now belongs to our Lord and to his Anointed, and he will reign forever and ever."

11:16 The twenty-four elders who sat on their thrones before God prostrated themselves and worshiped God

11:17 and said:
"We give thanks to you, Lord God almighty
who are and who were
For you have assumed your great power
and have established your reign.

11:18 The nations raged,
but your wrath has come,
and the time for the dead to be judged,
and to recompense your servants the prophets,
and the holy ones and those who fear your name,
the small and the great alike,
and to destroy those who destroy the earth."

11:19 Then God's temple in heaven was opened, and the ark of the covenant could be seen in the temple. There were flashes of lightning, rumblings, and peals of thunder, an earthquake, and a violent hailstorm.

In chapter 11's anticipation of the final trumpet blast (vv. 15–19), there is a continued treatment of the role of the prophet in the final days. Here, however, more than the words of the prophet, consideration is given to the role of the prophet as a witness or, in some cases, as a martyr.

In the temple vision (vv. 1–2), the inner temple represents the new Israel, which is preserved from desecration. The end-time community is itself the true temple (1 Cor 3:10,16). The outer temple court, or the court of the Gentiles, is given over to destruction. Again the two aspects of eschatology come to the fore: deliverance and destruction. Measure the temple *(v. 1): This is clearly an Ezekiel reference where the construction of the new post-exilic temple is predicted (40:3–42).* Forty-two months *(v. 2): This points to the three and one half years of punishment to be inflicted on the Jews during the reign of Antiochus Epiphanes (Dn 7:25; 12:7). These references are replete with eschatological overtones.*

The witnesses (martyrs) are better seen as a duo giving credible witness (Mt 18:16) rather than as a reference to concrete individuals, for example, Moses and Elijah. Sackcloth *(v. 3): Penitential attire.* Two olive trees and two lampstands *(v. 4): These are identified with the*

*two witnesses in an image drawn from Zechariah (4:1–3; 11–14).
There the kingly (Zerubbabel) and priestly (Joshua) "life giving" figures
are presented as olive trees providing oil for the lampstands. Here the
two prophetic witnesses provide a similar but broader service. They sup-
ply life and light to God's people as agents of God's Spirit. In the true
spirit of the prophets of old, the two witnesses can bring fire from heaven
or close the sky like Elijah (1 Kgs 18:36–40; 17:1) or change water into
blood like Moses (Ex 7:17–20).*

*At the end of their testimony the beast appears from the underworld (the
abyss), the great symbol of evil (Dn 7:2–8). He wages bloody warfare
against the prophets and wins (vv. 7–8).* Sodom...Egypt *(v. 8):
Symbolic names for the "great city," consistently seen as Rome in
Revelation. Sodom is biblically synonymous with corruption (Is 1:10);
Egypt was the country of oppression (Ex 1:11–14), akin to the violent
Jerusalem which killed the prophets and Christ himself. Both titles are easily applied to Rome. Thus both the beast and the city are symbolic of
Roman inhumanity.* Three and a half days *(v. 9): Again, as in verse 2,
the half of perfection (seven) is perfect evil (three and one half). The power
and sway of the beast are in control. The period of desolation is followed by
the vindication of the two prophets (vv. 11–13). They are raised from the
dead by a new life-giving spirit (Ez 37:10) and are taken to the heavenly
realm. Punishment ensues and leads some to conversion (v. 12).*

*Some authors feel that chapters 10–11, up to this point, are an
addenda to the original writing as a type of apotheosis on the role of
prophetic witness. This is admittedly hard to verify in view of the general nonsequential style of apocalyptic.*

The Seventh Trumpet (vv. 15–19)

*This is a glimpse of the final victory which will be developed in later
chapters, and this is also the last of the three predicted "woes" (9:12;
11:14). The "loud voices" which herald this breakthrough of God's
glory are unidentified (v. 15).*

Kingdom...he will reign *(v. 15): This points to the sovereignty of
God over the whole of creation, with the concurrent observance of his
will. It represents the overthrow of all secular and evil forces of domination in ushering in the era of grace and love.* We give thanks *(v. 16):
This is eucharistic language well known from the Didache, as well as*

the thanksgiving psalms of the psalter. As the chant of the twenty-four elders, this is a berakah *or recognition of the graciousness and favor of God. This is the God "who is" and "who was" with no mention of the future, since the era of the future is already present (v. 15). Once the beast and his minions are overthrown, then the overarching sovereignty of God will be established. It is the era of final judgment (v. 18) for both the living and the dead (v. 18), a moment of vindication for the "holy ones" (the saved, the elect) and the prophets.* Those who destroy the earth *(v. 18): Any inversion of the moral order affects an alienated earth as well (Rom 8:20–23). In this moment of exaltation and over-whelming theophany, the heavenly temple itself is thrown open (v. 19). In earthly times, the holiest place was a restricted area, with access granted only to the high priest on determined occasions. Now it becomes an "open door" in the clear sight of all. The ark, which had been lost after the destruction of the temple in the sixth century, is given an end-time restoration. As the footstool of the Lord, it is fittingly part of the final enthronement as lightning, thunder, and earthquake surround this eschatological moment of divine enthronement.*

WORSHIP AND WITNESS

With the sounding of the seventh trumpet, a scene of heavenly worship emerges centered on the temple and the elect of God. God is praised by the heavenly choir in openness before the temple and the ark, as the one who has obtained victory over the forces of evil. This paean of praise follows the account of the two witnesses, symbolic of all Christian prophets who have given their lives in testimony to the truth.

Worship is anything but peripheral in the Christian life; it stands at the very heart of the Judeo-Christian tradition. God is praised in *berakah* because of his overwhelming goodness in bonding with us, in saving us, in giving us an eternal destiny. This is all summarized in Eucharist, the re-presentation of Christ's saving death and resurrection. As a faith community, all our worship is centered on recognizing who God is and what he has done for us. Before any other consideration, our worship acknowledges the goodness of God publicly before the world. In the Eucharist we are co-worshipers with the Son in praise and glory to the Father. And the *anamnesis* ("in memory of me") remembers not only what Christ has done but is also a request to God to recall what his Son endured. It is small wonder that the Vatican Council saw the liturgy as the apogee of the Christian life. It is not just something that sets Sunday apart but rather the summation of our experience as Christians.

THE BODY OF BELIEVERS

It is the community that is placed in bold relief in the structure of the liturgy. The presider and the other ministers have very distinctive functions, but it is on the body of the faithful that the light focuses. This is not an attendance at mass where we are passive recipients of Word and sacrament. It is an active participation that engages the congregation; it is theirs to own in the fullest sense of the word. Even the priest, with his indispensable role, has clearly defined limits. Spatially his place is in the sanctuary; even at the exchange of peace, he is to greet only those around him, not the members of the congregation. It is his to preach the Word and to perform the sacred action, and he should be as reluctant to surrender the first as he would the second. The gathering song at the beginning is a communal praise of God, not a moment in which "we welcome our celebrant" as he moves toward the altar. It is even suggested that liturgically it is preferable for the presider to be already at his place before the hymn is sung. The basic idea centers on the primacy of the believing community in this central prayer of their life.

In the course of the liturgy various ministries come into play—communion ministers, lectors, servers—all pointing up the communal and ecclesial character of what transpires. Like the presider, they are at the service of the community, the Eucharist being a microcosm of what service in the Christian community means. Social ministries center on the Eucharist, draw their strength and inspiration from it, and become a prolongation of its basic spirit. To the altar we bring our hopes, worries, and human difficulties; from the altar we draw the example of the self-giving Christ and are fortified in the Spirit to go and do likewise. How little we understand all this whenever we frame our

Sunday worship in terms of "obligation." Or we view its omission in terms of mortal or venial sin. The truth is that the Eucharist is privilege, grace, the heartfelt response of a grateful people. To see it simply in terms of duty is to miss the point. It is not something we fit into our Sunday; rather it makes our Sunday, indeed our entire week. We are part of Revelation's heavenly choir, which endlessly praises God in his sovereignty and goodness.

TOTAL EQUALITY

The high priest of the earlier covenant entered the Most Holy Place, the inner part of the temple, once a year. And he alone did so. The general congregation never entered this sacred zone where the ark of the covenant was located. But Christ, our high priest, has entered the heavenly sanctuary once and for all, as the Epistle to the Hebrews states. He has done this with his saving death and has thus gained access for us all. We have therefore been constituted a "royal priesthood, a holy people"; and thus in this great vision of Revelation, God's heavenly temple is thrown open, and the ark is clearly visible to all. With the death of Christ in the Matthean Gospel, the separating veil of the temple is rent from top to bottom (27:51), thus giving definitive access to all of the elect. There is no exclusivity in this final era in which we live. God finds equally acceptable the little and the great. It is one Lord, one faith, one baptism. There are no elite in the reign of God.

In a world that underscores the importance of political correctness, that never ceases to make exceptions, and that applauds rank and privilege, Christians should be indeed counter-cultural. How many people are bypassed on the highway of life! When we think of all the people so easily overlooked, the scriptures remind us that before God we are all of equal stature, and if there be any preference at all, it is directed toward the weakest of the world. Each Sunday the richest and the poorest approach the altar with equal rights and recognition. The only royal status is that of our common priesthood.

Yet all of this has to be translated into action as a program of life. As eucharistic people, we must face the question of whether or not we are truly open and accepting. Is it the wealthy and famous whom we are anxious to cultivate? Or are we equally at home with those who by human standards count for little? We say we are not prejudiced, racist, or biased. The word is out today that discrimination is by no means dead. We may no longer have churches where white and black are separated, but is this matched by personal attitudes of openness to people of a different race? Yes, a sense of equality and concern for the less fortunate is emblazoned on the pages of the scriptures, but we are still hierarchical in our thinking. Frequently one hears, "If the pope doesn't have a direct line to God, who does?" The answer is, "You do!" Together we approach the throne of God with Christ our brother. Because this people is so sacred, some of us are called as servants and ministers to provide for their needs. The people do not exist for the ministers of the church, but just the opposite. The New Testament could not be clearer.

UNWELCOME PROPHETS

The two witnesses of chapter 11 represent the prophets of the church but can easily be identified with the prophets of the Old Testament as well. Prophecy all too frequently has led to martyrdom, even in modern times. A prophet is primarily a mouthpiece of the Lord, one who speaks a message that all too often runs counter to popular thought. Despite the fact that times and cultures have identified themselves as religious or borne the name "Christian," the radical call of the gospel has torn the fabric of a complacent, undisturbed way of life. As much as we may try to tame that call into acceptable domesticity, the demands remain inescapable. It has often meant death for its adherents. To live Christian principle in the face of opposition even to death leads to a double title: confessor (prophet) and martyr. It says that there are values beyond the present which are worth more than life itself. These witnesses to the unassailable truth extend from the apostles to Maximilian Kolbe and Oscar Romero.

There are and have been Christian prophets who address the church itself. But how easily they can be dismissed because they are not dealing with civil evils but those within a sacred institution. The Dominican friar Girolamo Savonarola called for a thoroughgoing reform of the church in the early sixteenth century. He decried many of the abuses within the church that would be echoed by Martin Luther only a few years later. But by the time of Luther it was too late. The church was ripe for division.

In Florence, Savonarola paid dearly for his strong convictions, which were much too disturbing for Florentine society and the institutional church. He died at the hands of a "Christian" society. Had he been heeded, immense damage might have been avoided. Today there are calls for him to be named a saint by a repentant church. In our own times, there are honest and dedicated people who call for a reform of life and structures within the church, and they do it from a deep sense of conviction. But it is all too easy to dismiss them as "fringe Catholics" or fault-finders. But the fact is that we all have much to learn from a careful hearing. In many aspects of its life the church is human and therefore reformable. Perhaps we accept that truth more willingly in theory than in fact.

After their martyrdom the prophets of revelation heard the voice from above saying, "Come up here." We have to believe that ultimately the truth will triumph. If evil is to have the last word, then we are mercilessly deceived. As a Jewish rabbi friend said to me: "Even after Auschwitz I *have* to believe." The cause of God is the cause of right, and if faith means anything, then the justice of God must triumph. This is in our heart every time we stand at a bedside and hold the hand of a person torn by pain. Or when we see the weapons of war poised for destruction or the mines hidden in a field only waiting for the step of the unknowing. We believe when we hold in silence a mother who has lost a child in unforeseen ways. The prophets believed in the victory of God. They were not always heard, but they spoke the word of truth. Pain has always been their lot. But we would be much poorer without them.

Reflections on Worship and Prophecy

1. Worship, as the prayer of the church, brings us close to God in many ways. Do I see it in that light or simply as a Sunday obligation?

2. Prophecy plays a major role in Revelation. In what way does it touch my life?

3. Biblical prophets address princes and priests. Can we appreciate modern prophets who address both church and state?

4. The heavenly temple is completely open. How does that differ from the Jewish temple?

5. Who are the present-day "destroyers of the earth"?

THE BATTLE REVISITED (12:1–18)

THE WOMAN AND THE DRAGON

12:1 **A great sign appeared in the sky, a woman clothed with the sun, with the moon under her feet, and on her head a crown of twelve stars.**

12:2 **She was with child and wailed aloud in pain as she labored to give birth.**

12:3 **Then another sign appeared in the sky; it was a huge red dragon, with seven heads and ten horns, and on its heads were seven diadems.**

12:4 **Its tail swept away a third of the stars in the sky and hurled them down to the earth. Then the dragon stood before the woman about to give birth, to devour her child when she gave birth.**

12:5 **She gave birth to a son, a male child, destined to rule all the nations with an iron rod. Her child was caught up to God and his throne.**

12:6 **The woman herself fled into the desert where she had a place prepared by God, that there she might be taken care of for twelve hundred and sixty days.**

12:7 **Then war broke out in heaven; Michael and his angels battled against the dragon. The dragon and its angels fought back,**

12:8 **but they did not prevail and there was no longer any place for them in heaven.**

12:9 **The huge dragon, the ancient serpent, who is called the Devil and Satan, who deceived the whole world, was thrown down to earth, and its angels were thrown down with it.**

12:10 Then I heard a loud voice in heaven say:
"Now have salvation and power come,
    and the kingdom of our God
    and the authority of his Anointed.
For the accuser of our brothers is cast out,
    who accuses them before our God day and night.

12:11 They conquered him by the blood of the Lamb
    and by the word of their testimony;
    love for life did not deter them from death.

12:12 Therefore, rejoice, you heavens,
    and you who dwell in them.
But woe to you, earth and sea,
    for the Devil has come down to you in great fury,
    for he knows he has but a short time."

12:13 When the dragon saw that it had been thrown down to the earth, it pursued the woman who had given birth to the male child.

12:14 But the woman was given the two wings of the great eagle, so that she could fly to her place in the desert, where, far from the serpent, she was taken care of for a year, two years, and a half-year.

12:15 The serpent, however, spewed a torrent of water out of his mouth after the woman to sweep her away with the current.

12:16 But the earth helped the woman and opened its mouth and swallowed the flood that the dragon spewed out of its mouth.

12:17 Then the dragon became angry with the woman and went off to wage war against the rest of her offspring, those who keep God's commandments and bear witness to Jesus.

12:18 It took its position on the sand of the sea.

The account of the woman and the dragon can be read against the background of two known mythologies. The first is Greek and deals with the birth of a god who is faced with the threat of destruction by an evil force. The god was Apollo, whose mother Leto fled to the island of Delos (near

Patmos) to escape the dragon Python. This son of Zeus lives and eventually destroys the dragon. The second is the well-known myth of the cosmic battle between good and evil, depicted in terms of angels and evil monsters. There are biblical accounts of evil agents anxious to become Godlike who are ultimately thrown down (Is 14:13–15; Ez 28:11–19).

In chapter 12, it is important to identify the principal actors:

- The woman *is Israel-Church, which gives birth to the Messiah. She is adorned with sun, moon, and stars, representative of the patriarchal Israel (Gn 37:9–10). She is likened to Eve, the mother of the living, who brings forth children in travail (Gn 3:16; Is 66:7–14).*

- The child *is clearly the Messiah, "a son, a male child, destined to rule the nations (Is 66:7; Gn 49:10). There is mention of his salvific passing from earth to heaven in his death-resurrection (v. 5).*

- Michael and the angels *head up the cosmic battle. Michael assumes his role as the protector of God's people (Dn 10:13; 12:1).*

- The dragon *is here the symbol of all evil, identified as Satan, the adversary, by this point being termed clearly the devil (2 Cor 12:7; 2 Thes 2:9). He is also the serpent of Genesis (v. 9; Gn 3:1–14). He has* ten horns, *here also identified with imperial power (Dn 7:24; 7:7),* seven diadems *(authority), and* seven heads.

- The battle. *It is to be noted that this does not carry the story line forward, but is a re-presentation of the conflict already reported. The dragon is poised to destroy the Messiah (v. 4). But the Christ is delivered and taken up to God. The woman (Israel-Church) remains in a desert place (Exodus theme) for a limited period of persecution (1,260 days = forty-two months = three and one-half years), the biblical period of trial and desolation (Dn 7:25; 8:14).*

The scene shifts to the battle itself (vv. 7–9). The satanic forces in heaven lose and are cast to earth. The dragon then turns to attack the woman, but on eagles' wings (Ex 19:4; Dt 32:11) she is borne aloft and carried to an idyllic desert place, to be protected during the final travail (three and one-half years). It should be noted that any attempts to base a belief on evil's origins in terms of the fallen angels of this chapter would have to reckon with the apocalyptic genre is which it is expressed.

The continuing persecution by the dragon/serpent, which spews forth a deluge of enmity, would be seen by the people of John's time as the sustained attacks against Christians under Nero (v. 15). The earth is the battlefield of this conflict, but it too is destined to be finally redeemed (c. 21; Rom 8:19–28). There is a transition from war waged against the church as a whole to conflict with the individual Christian (v. 17).

It took its position *(v. 18): The dragon is positioned near the sea, the site of one of evil's habitats (13:1). Some later manuscripts read "I took my stand"* (Gr.: estathen), *thus relating it to the opening of the next chapter.*

The Hymn (vv. 10–12)

Victory is acclaimed in light of the "accuser's" (Satan's) overthrowal (v. 10), following his being thrown to earth. Thus, to the former attributes given to God another is added: savior or salvation (Gr.: soteria). *The reign of God is coupled with the authority or sovereignty given now to Christ in light of his death-resurrection (Acts 2:36). Satan is depicted as an accuser here (Jb 1:9–11), one who strives to sever the bond between God and believers, but he cannot succeed (Rom 8:33–35).*

Christians are now vindicated (v. 11). Redeemed by the blood of Christ, they have triumphed not only in baptism but by the witness of their lives (word of their testimony) even to the point of martyrdom.

Finally, the acclamation of praise goes out to the heavenly court, where the saved will reign; and the dirge of woe is directed to the earth, where Satan will continue to wreak his havoc for a limited period of time.

THE WOMAN AND THE DRAGON

It would help immensely if life were always as clear as the black and white issues of Revelation. When good and evil are depicted in terms of a beautiful woman adorned with a heavenly constellation and a voracious tail-sweeping dragon, it is not too difficult to determine which side we would choose. But the heart of this chapter points to the timeless struggle between the powers of heaven and those of hell. And as experience indicates so well, we are anything but bystanders in this ongoing struggle. In this chapter it goes between heaven and earth; in our life it goes between time and eternity. It is both institutional and deeply personal.

If we look at the church in history, the imagery of Revelation could easily be interpreted in terms of the countless struggles the church has had with "Caesar" over the centuries. It goes back to the early Roman persecutions alluded to in Revelation itself. The church of the so-called Dark Ages and the Middle Ages saw itself not only as a spiritual force but a major political one as well. Every major European power from Constantine to Charlemagne and Frederick the Great, and then on to Napoleon and Bismarck, had to deal with the pope as a major secular power. The unification of Italy in the nineteenth century and the end of the papal states ended most of this, and as painful as this event might have been, it proved ultimately to be a great blessing for the church. More than once during this long period the woman and the dragon were seen as engaged in mortal conflict, with the identification of the respective figures largely dependent on where one stood in the ordeal. In a different form, this end-time struggle has marked much of the twentieth century as well, as war clouds have gathered on the horizons repeatedly during the past hundred years.

On religious issues, the same dichotomy has emerged and reemerged. Certainly in some Catholic eyes, the reformers of the sixteenth century were seen as demonic perverters of the church. The woman was the Catholic Church engaged in mortal conflict with the heretical dragon. In the reformers' outlook, the dragon, as well as later beasts and unseemly people of Revelation, was seen as the Catholic Church waging a spiritual war against those who had fled her domain of spiritual and political control in search of a more scripture-centered Christianity. All the evils of the Inquisition epitomized the spewing dragon at its worst. And so Revelation was variously interpreted largely in terms of embattled figures or institutions being reckoned as the guilty or innocent parties. In all of this there was undoubtedly some of the woman and some of the dragon on both sides.

It is important to realize that the dragon is not always an external force. It can be as internal to the church as it can be to each one of us. And at that point it becomes so personal that it is very difficult to draw the line. *Ecclesia semper reformanda.* The church is in need of constant and ongoing reform. The church's spiritual character and mission are encased in humanity, and therefore in weakness as well as strength. In theory it all sounds fine; the problem lies in deciding what needs reform and who the reformers will be. The dragon must be cast down, but identifying it is not always easy. When some call for the reform of certain structures in the church, the champions of the status quo defend their position in God's name. The reformers are labeled as woefully ill informed or even insolent. The reformers, for their part, often see the champions of the achieved position as entrenched bureaucrats who show little concern for God's people or the signs of the times.

It is interesting to look at the contrary points of view that swirl around liturgical renewal so many years after the Vatican Council. It is said that the dragon to be exorcised has appeared on both sides and the question of its being "cast out" hinges on perspective. As to the question of language in liturgy, the literalist will say that the Vatican Council envisioned a limited amount of the vernacular in the mass but wanted Latin to be retained; others, probably the great majority, argue that an ongoing interpretation of the conciliar texts led the church ultimately to approve a total use of the vernacular in the sacraments. And honesty compels us to admit that there is some truth in both positions. But instead of reaching accord in this and in many other matters, the dragon and the woman, in an ambiguous way, continue to be in conflict. It might certainly be argued that the church itself is in the best position to decide the "spirit of the council" and did so in amplifying the use of the vernacular. But there are still those who will say that this was accomplished through the machinations of people on the inner circles of decision making and was a wholly human and one-sided decision. The result is that instead of having one dragon we now have two—the outer circle decision makers and the inner circle manipulators.

What happens as a result? In the midst of such ambiguity there is no victory, there is only an impasse. There is an abrupt halt to all new forms of liturgical renewal. There is an amplification of the Latin mass, not only in its reformed rite, but also its earlier Tridentine form, that is, the mass of fifty years ago. Attempts to make the language of the liturgy more inclusive are looked at askance. The inclusion of young women as altar servers is seen as an advancement of the feminist agenda. On the other side, New Age liturgies appear, which celebrate the Earth or the eternal feminine. Prayer and liturgy become more agenda-driven and appeal to an ever more limited audience. In all of this, who are the "cops" and who are the "robbers"? Who is the dragon and who is the woman? It is quite true that the great majority of people find themselves in a rather well-defined middle ground. But the tensions of right and left persist like a housefly on a hot summer afternoon.

In so many instances the objectivity of apocalyptic is not easy to find. When the mindset is already in place, reality is invariably viewed through that prism. Just as there were Catholics who saw the Protestant reform as the great dragon, there were Protestants who saw Catholics in the same terms. Unfortunately the polarization that exists within the Catholic Church today convinces us that the situation is not much different. If the church is to be "continually reformed," it will take a determined effort to listen and learn and to move away from our predeterminations.

THE PERSONAL SIDE

"I say, then: live by the Spirit and you will certainly not gratify the desire of the flesh. For the flesh has desires against the Spirit, and the Spirit against the flesh; these are opposed to each other, so that you may not do what you want" (Gal 5:16–17). Flesh and spirit; dragon and woman. It is useless for us to speak of the competing opposites in the world around us or in the church if we fail to speak of it within ourselves. When we consider how poorly we respond to this polarity in our personal lives, we should not be surprised that the church as a whole does not quite measure up either. The fact is that we are all light and shadow, good news and bad news, Jekyll and Hyde. There are moments in which we sense the presence of God so strongly in our lives that our faith seems indomitable. It may be a deeply felt liturgy, a cursillo or some retreat experience, a hospital visit, or some keenly felt experience of the arts. We have never felt more in touch with God or more positive about ourselves. But it is amazing how quickly that can change. Some weakness in our makeup causes us to fall from the heights and to grovel in a deep feeling of alienation. The passage is sometimes so abrupt that we can hardly continue to believe in ourselves. It may be any number of things. That first drink that we knew would be our downfall, that unnoticed cheating, that sexual attraction that seemed just too strong to resist. And then guilt sets in (which is not necessarily a bad thing) and makes us feel our unworthiness, our grime and dirt, our betrayal. It is safe to say that there are very few of us who have not experienced this at some time in our life. We start with the woman clothed with the sun and end with the dragon spewing his hatred upon the earth. We are an immense disappointment to ourselves. And if anybody would learn this, we would be totally humiliated.

But in this era of history, wherein the end time is still working itself out, we are not lost. The eschatological battle in Revelation is quickly fought and finished. Not so in the way it is worked out in life. "It's not over till the fat lady sings." And for us that means until we breathe our last. If we have seen the dragon, we are better disposed to adhere to the lady crowned with the sun. She does represent the church in Revelation, and through baptism we belong to her and she to us. She, no less than we, has had her time of desolation, three and a half years. But she does not fail. Neither should we. It is only when we read Revelation realistically that we can grasp its message. Yes, there is sin and there is evil in the world, and there is some of that in all of us. But the message of Revelation is not one of defeat but one of victory. The ultimate outcome is positive. Let us learn from our mistakes; let us never call evil good; but let us never lose confidence in the belief that we too will conquer "by the blood of the Lamb." Know sin, avoid it; it belongs to the dragon and the underworld; it has an unmistakable stench. We need only reflection and conversion. But the Father and the Lamb are always there to see us through.

There is no doubt about the fact that the dragon is present in our world today. The basic values of Christianity are repeatedly discarded in public and private life. Even more disturbing is the general malaise or indifference to religion that so permeates Western culture. There are the life and death issues, the problems of economic depression and discrimination, the culture of materialism, to mention but a few. All require a truly Christian response, but one that is thoughtful, studied, and prayerful.

The heart of the woman-dragon discussion is one of division. But we cannot end on a negative note. We cannot forget the important strides toward unity that have marked the churches and world religions over many years, especially since the council ended. Many issues that formerly divided the Christian churches have moved toward solution; the climate of understanding today among the churches is better than at any time since the Reformation. The opportunities to speak today with a unified voice are more numerous than they have ever been. Science and religion have partnered in many ways. We have not yet really measured the results of the Vatican Council; they have outrun all of us. The question of religious liberty is resolved once and for all, as well as the recognition of other churches as true ecclesial bodies. We have pledged ourselves to fight antisemitism and to recognize our common bonds with the Jewish people. We recognize the good that is present in the great world religions. These are all reminders that division is never insurmountable—if we can only change and grow. "The Evil One knows that he has but a short time" (12:12). For us evil is not an eternal principle; the Lamb and the One seated on the throne are destined to triumph. This is the clear teaching of Revelation, a teaching we cannot forget.

THE TWO BEASTS (13:1–18)

THE FIRST BEAST

13:1 **Then I saw a beast come out of the sea with ten horns and seven heads; on its horns were ten diadems, and on its heads blasphemous name[s].**

13:2 **The beast I saw was like a leopard, but it had feet like a bear's, and its mouth was like the mouth of a lion. To it the dragon gave its own power and throne, along with great authority.**

13:3 I saw that one of its heads seemed to have been mortally wounded, but this mortal wound was healed. Fascinated, the whole world followed after the beast.

13:4 They worshiped the dragon because it gave its authority to the beast; they also worshiped the beast and said, "Who can compare with the beast or who can fight against it?"

13:5 The beast was given a mouth uttering proud boasts and blasphemies, and it was given authority to act for forty-two months.

13:6 It opened its mouth to utter blasphemies against God, blaspheming his name and his dwelling and those who dwell in heaven.

13:7 It was also allowed to wage war against the holy ones and conquer them, and it was granted authority over every tribe, people, tongue, and nation.

13:8 All the inhabitants of the earth will worship it, all whose names were not written from the foundation of the world in the book of life, which belongs to the Lamb who was slain.

13:9 Whoever has ears ought to hear these words.

13:10 Anyone destined for captivity goes into captivity.
    Anyone destined to be slain by the sword shall be slain by
       the sword.
Such is the faithful endurance of the holy ones.

THE SECOND BEAST

13:11 Then I saw another beast come up out of the earth; it had two horns like a lamb's but spoke like a dragon.

13:12 It wielded all the authority of the first beast in its sight and made the earth and its inhabitants worship the first beast, whose mortal wound had been healed.

13:13 It performed great signs, even making fire come down from heaven to earth in the sight of everyone.

13:14 It deceived the inhabitants of the earth with the signs it was allowed to perform in the sight of the first beast, telling them to make an image for the beast who had been wounded by the sword and revived.

13:15 It was then permitted to breathe life into the beast's image, so that the beast's image could speak and [could] have anyone who did not worship it put to death.

13:16 It forced all the people, small and great, rich and poor, free and slave, to be given a stamped image on their right hands or their foreheads,

13:17 so that no one could buy or sell except one who had the stamped image of the beast's name or the number that stood for its name.

13:18 Wisdom is needed here; one who understands can calculate the number of the beast, for it is a number that stands for a person. His number is six hundred and sixty-six.

Operative text: Daniel 7:2–8.
History: the chapter deals with the period of Nero and later Domitian (A.D. 81–96).
The first beast receives its authority from the dragon (Satan) (v. 4). Here the evil force is concretized historically in the Roman Empire. Just as Roman military force came from the Mediterranean, the beast too emerges out of the sea (v. 1). Ten horns *(v. 1): Daniel 7:8.20; Revelation 17:12–14.* Seven heads *(v. 1): Either the seven hills of Rome or the seven major emperors.* Blasphemous names *(v. 1): Divine names accorded the emperor, as* divus, augustus, dominus, deus. Leopard, bear, lion *(v. 2): In Daniel these are separate beasts; here they coalesce into one. Notice the unusual imagery: beast with seven heads but one mouth.* Wounded head *(v. 3): This seemingly refers to Nero, who died after a self-inflicted wound (A.D. 68) and whose expected postmortem return was a popular belief.*
Some interesting likenesses emerge between the Lamb and the beast (Nero). Just as the Lamb receives the scroll and his authority from above (5:7,12), so the beast receives his from the dragon (v. 2). The Lamb's rule extends to every tribe, and language (5:9); so does the beast's (v. 7). One receives heavenly homage (5:7), the other, earthly (v. 4). Both the Lamb (5:6) and the beast (v. 3) bear their mortal wounds. This parallel

between the two kingdoms underscores striking differences in a paradoxical way, perhaps with a note of sarcasm.

The activity of the beast is primarily expressed in oral terms (vv. 5–6), uttering blasphemies such as designating Caesar as divine (Dn 7:8). Forty-two months *(v. 5): Again limits are placed on the era of evil, that is, three and one-half years. All the nations of the earth worship the beast, except the Christians, who are being persecuted (vv. 7–8). The admonition counsels nonretaliation on the part of the Christians (vv. 9–10). In suffering with a spirit of endurance* (Gr.: upomone), *they will be ultimately vindicated, even though the present means only suffering and death.*

The second beast (vv. 11–18) comes from the land, with two horns and dragon speech. At this point the trinity of evil is complete, with the dragon and two beasts. As the first beast was subordinate to the dragon, so the second is subordinate to the first beast. If the first beast is identified as Nero, the second is elsewhere seen as s false prophet (16:13; 19:20; 20:10), that is, a promoter or emissary of the great evil, the Roman Empire. False prophets were capable of great wonders (Dt 13:2–4), and the New Testament predicts their appearance (Mt 24:24; Mk 13:22; 2 Thes 2:9). But they are ultimately deceived; they operate from illusion.

The speaking statue (vv. 14–17) is hard to pinpoint. Greek literature speaks of moving and talking statues in the Hierapolis temple. Here it is concerned with emperor worship being promoted by imperial emissaries (the false prophets). The worship of the emperor in statue form is central here, and the statue "speaks" in as much as imperial forces enforce the will of the emperor. Failure to pay homage meant death. Those who did not conform (that is, did not receive the clear stamp of the emperor) were stricken from commerce and were not able to sustain a livelihood.

666 *(v. 18): This numerical symbol of evil has had no shortage of designated candidates from the pope to Hitler. Generically it could simply stand for perfect evil: seven is the number of perfection; six, a deficient number, is symbolic of evil. In Revelation, six plagues, six trumpets, and six seals were all major end-time disasters. In the context, however, the author is thinking of a concrete person. With the Hebrew letters of the two words* Nero Caesar *given their numerical value, addition gives 666–in Hebrew, however, not in Greek. We are certainly on safe ground in seeing the number as expressive of perfect evil; and in context Nero is certainly the beast.*

RENDER TO CAESAR

Jesus had a much more benign attitude toward Roman authority than did the author of Revelation. The latter is faced with organized persecution and an ongoing hostility that placed the infant church in danger of extinction. He is confident that such will not occur, that ultimately the victory of the Lamb will be evident, but in the meantime the gulf that exists between the elect and the forces of evil, variously described as dragon, beast, or whore, is wide and deep.

When Jesus is asked about the legality of paying Roman taxes (Mt 22:15–21), his answer is almost noncommittal. The question, as Jesus views it, has nothing to do with the reign of God. In requesting that he be shown the coin and asking whose image appears thereon, he is willing to leave temporalities on the level of completely human consideration. If government provides benefits of any type, then the money to pay for them must come from some source, logically from those who are beneficiaries. But all of that has no more to do with the reign of God than does the brand of breakfast food one eats. If you use roads, pay for them! It is there that Jesus' comment on civil authority begins and ends. And it should be added that if there ever were a conflict between the state and the demands of God, there is no doubt as to where allegiance should be centered.

And it is precisely to that area of irreconcilable claims that Revelation directs its attention. The Roman emperor was not only respected, he was worshiped. Rome made no distinction between the temporal and spiritual spheres. Allegiance was total, and failure to give Caesar his due in the order of temporalities or cult was nothing short of traitorous. This left the early Christian no option. One stood either with the Lamb or with the beast.

CIVIL MORALITY

In our day and age the situation is more ambiguous and certainly less clear. In a constitutional democracy we are responsible for an elected government, both in its legislative and executive functions. We may not be content with some of our elected officials, but we can be reasonably certain that their constituency is.

People are usually elected because of their real or alleged convictions, which may or may not be compatible with the views of the public at large. This means that we play the cards we are dealt. And not infrequently the positions of elected officials are directly at variance with our religious and moral sentiments. This can and should create genuine problems of conscience. In such instances, how is it possible to render to Caesar...?

When we look at the good that government can and often does accomplish, we realize that we are not simply dealing with the ugly beast of Revelation. Government often does help the needy and the unemployed, come to the aid of people in the face of widespread catastrophe, provide health services according to need, and in different ways show compassion and sensitivity. But it can also act with a moral indifference that is detrimental to society and offensive to many of its citizens. Nothing stands out more clearly today than the relationship of government to the life issues. The protection of life from the womb to the tomb is viewed by many as a natural right, especially in the case of the most vulnerable; it is not primarily a religious issue. And therefore whenever religious bodies raise their voice in a democratic society, it is not an attempt to impose religious beliefs on others; it is simply asking the state to adhere to its fundamental *raison d'être*. When it fails to do so, it assumes the features of the apocalyptic beast.

There is, for example, the whole question of war, and the legitimate question as to whether or not limitations can be imposed to speak of a war as being "just." Before there can be any taking of life, be it that of combatant or noncombatant, there must be a sufficiently grave reason. Christian pacifism, which has deep biblical roots, would argue that any taking of life is contrary to Christ's teaching. But in the event of a "less than Christian" response to a military threat, there is the clear danger of a type of military buildup to precipitate a response far beyond the limits of anything legitimate or acceptable. There is also the proliferation of weapons and their sale to other national powers. In the interests of national security, many actions are sanctioned that are clearly at odds with religious principle. We should be thankful for prophetic voices, as thankless as their task often is. We need honesty in our society. Just as the second beast performed deceptive signs on behalf of the first beast in chapter 13, so too there are those who persuade an uninformed public of the reasons for government actions. But the Lamb too must have prophets. We should listen and not muffle their voices.

And what of our widespread materialism and greed? The insatiable thirst for profit that motivates so much of commerce and business? The beast is there as well. This is particularly evident in the fortunes that are made through the illegal promotion of drugs, widespread pornography and organized crime. They are lethal to the moral makeup of society, and we are the losers in simply coming to terms with them. If the Book of Revelation is clear on anything, it is on calling evil by name. In the imagery used and the polarized interfacing of good and evil, we are left with no uncertainty. Today, however, clarity becomes obscurity, as we attempt to adapt and qualify, not in those areas where things are by nature not that clear, but rather in those which are born of an exaggerated relativism. Such is to give the beast an upper hand.

FORMS OF RESISTANCE

In the midst of the presentation of the two beasts, there is an encomium, unidentified as to its source, highlighting the holy ones of God. If destined for imprisonment, to prison they shall go. If destined for martyrdom, slain they shall be. The question is raised: Does this echo the nonresistance to evil about which the gospel speaks? It is the term *endurance* that emerges repeatedly, a concept to which Paul returns often in his letters. To respond to evil with evil is simply to unleash moral violence. It results in a chain of unimpeded wrongdoing, leaving in its wake chaos and death. Self-defense is a legitimate response to a life threat, but there are clear limits to such a response. Endurance is a virtue that is all too seldom held up to view, because it means silent suffering. Countless people in world history have been its champion in suffering for years because of conviction. In every culture, under numerous regimes in the course of history, people were silenced either through death or through detention, often done surreptitiously. Imprisonment has all too often taken the form of torture and severe maltreatment. How often have we heard accounts of twenty, thirty, even forty years of imprisonment for reasons of conscience? Do we imagine what it means to be deprived of the basic goods of life—home, family, friends, and work—for the greater part of a lifetime? It is a sobering and painful thought.

Endurance means confinement in very close quarters, a diet that has no semblance of being appetizing, an absence of companionship and conversation. Part of the punishment is a compulsory solitude. Day follows day in endless monotony, with little or nothing to occupy the mind. When we realize what freedom of movement signifies—the ability to grow and to help others grow, to help build the mind and spirit, to worship and assemble—and then consider being deprived of all of this for years on end, at that point we may begin to realize why the scriptures speak of endurance as holy.

Yet endurance breaks the chain of evil reprisal. It gathers the pain into oneself and allows it to go no further. It effectively blocks the boomerang quality of violence and puts it to rest in the pain and suffering often known only to God. To meet violence with violence is to find ourselves in a culture of death. The death penalty in society is a response to evil that only continues the chain of violence. Most of Western civilization today realizes that truth and does not see it as a solution. To take a life for a life reflects an ancient ethic of an "eye for an eye," which for Christians has been superseded in the teaching of Jesus. Our level of conscience should have risen to realize that human life is sacred at all stages. To choose execution over life imprisonment is to make the state an agent of death, and therefore to some degree a collaborator in the very thing that it deplores. Certainly there are varying degrees of culpability, but a civil government that provides for life in countless ways, from food and drug laws to traffic lights, fails in consistency when it becomes an agent of death. This is not the role of a humanizing, life-giving society. It is true that the interests of justice must be served and fitting punishment administered for serious crime. But in life not everything works out in perfect balance. Endurance may call us to suffer loss in a way that leaves the human scale unbalanced. But we suffer it because of our aversion for the taking of life and a deep-seated will not to respond in kind.

This teaching is never easy. We are called to endure in countless painful ways. Some years ago, a personal acquaintance, a priest in one of our large metropolitan areas, lost his elderly mother through inflicted violence. A thief broke into her home one evening and killed her in the course of a routine robbery. For years it weighed heavily on the priest, who could not reconcile his hostile feelings with his Christian convictions. The murderer was tried and sentenced to prison. The priest bore his own pain in silence over many years. But he returned to the issue time after time in personal prayer and in preaching forgiveness. Christ's call for total forgiveness was like the stab of conscience. Preparing to preach forgiveness once again on a given Sunday, he knew that he could no longer preach authentically. He called and made an appointment to meet the perpetrator in prison. They were reconciled, and a new chapter in the priest's life began. It is an inspiring story that could be retold in the lives of countless people. Endurance. We should reflect on its meaning more than we do.

From the Devil to Church and State

1. In general, how do you see church–state relations in the Bible? What was the authority of each?

2. Retribution and endurance seem to be values in conflict. Would you agree?

3. Discuss some of the ways in which the woman of chapter 12 has been viewed historically.

4. How are salvation and "the blood of the lamb" entwined in Revelation?

5. How did the devil originate? What is his biblical role?

6. Speak in modern terms of the war between the devil and the woman's offspring.

7. How does Revelation view the splendor and glory of Rome?

8. What are some of the ways in which 666 has been interpreted?

9. What does it mean to be stamped as a believer?

THE GREAT HARVEST (14:1–20)

THE LAMB'S COMPANIONS

14:1 Then I looked and there was the Lamb standing on Mount Zion, and with him a hundred and forty-four thousand who had his name and his Father's name written on their foreheads.

14:2 I heard a sound from heaven like the sound of rushing water or a loud peal of thunder. The sound I heard was like that of harpists playing their harps.

14:3 They were singing [what seemed to be] a new hymn before the throne, before the four living creatures and the elders. No one could learn this hymn except the hundred and forty-four thousand who had been ransomed from the earth.

14:4 These are they who were not defiled with women; they are virgins and these are the ones who follow the Lamb wherever he goes. They have been ransomed as the firstfruits of the human race for God and the Lamb.

14:5 On their lips no deceit has been found; they are unblemished.

THE THREE ANGELS

14:6 Then I saw another angel flying high overhead, with everlasting good news to announce to those who dwell on earth, to every nation, tribe, tongue, and people.

14:7 He said in a loud voice, "Fear God and give him glory, for his time has come to sit in judgment. Worship him who made heaven and earth and sea and springs of water."

14:8 A second angel followed, saying:
"Fallen, fallen is Babylon the great,
    that made all the nations drink
    the wine of her licentious passion."

14:9 A third angel followed them and said in a loud voice, "Anyone who worships the beast or its image, or accepts its mark on forehead or hand,

14:10 will also drink the wine of God's fury, poured full strength into the cup of his wrath, and will be tormented in burning sulfur before the holy angels and before the Lamb.

14:11 The smoke of the fire that torments them will rise forever and ever, and there will be no relief day or night for those who worship the beast or its image or accept the mark of its name."

14:12 Here is what sustains the holy ones who keep God's commandments and their faith in Jesus.

14:13 I heard a voice from heaven say, "Write this: Blessed are the dead who die in the Lord from now on." "Yes," said the Spirit, "let them find rest from their labors, for their works accompany them."

THE HARVEST OF THE EARTH

14:14 Then I looked and there was a white cloud, and sitting on the cloud one who looked like a son of man, with a gold crown on his head and a sharp sickle in his hand.

14:15 Another angel came out of the temple, crying out in a loud voice to the one sitting on the cloud, "Use your sickle and reap the harvest, for the time to reap has come, because the earth's harvest is fully ripe."

14:16 So the one who was sitting on the cloud swung his sickle over the earth, and the earth was harvested.

14:17 Then another angel came out of the temple in heaven who also had a sharp sickle.

14:18 Then another angel [came] from the altar, [who] was in charge of the fire, and cried out in a loud voice to the one who had the sharp sickle, "Use your sharp sickle and cut the clusters from the earth's vines, for its grapes are ripe."

14:19 So the angel swung his sickle over the earth and cut the earth's vintage. He threw it into the great wine press of God's fury.

14:20 The wine press was trodden outside the city and blood poured out of the wine press to the height of a horse's bridle for two hundred miles.

The Disciples of the Lamb (vv. 1-5)

Before the harvest of judgment occurs, we are given a preview of final victory, the triumph of the Lamb and his followers. This is another example of the juxtaposition of the negative (punishment) and the positive (deliverance). Mount Zion *(v. 1): Historically the place of God's dwelling in Jerusalem; here it is used transcendently as an eschatological venue (Jl 3:5). The elect (144,000) have been sealed with the names of both Christ and the Father (v. 1), in striking contrast to the citizens of the earthly realm who had been similarly stamped (13:16f). It is the elect alone who can learn the new hymn; it becomes another mark of their salvation.*

Virgins *(v. 4): The term is used here in a figurative sense. They have not been guilty of idolatry, which is biblically compared to fornication or adultery (Hos 2:4–21: Jer 2:2–6). These men and women who are saved are the ecclesial "spotless bride" (Eph 5:27). This also is connected with the celibate state being proper to the heavenly realm (Lk 20:34–36). The author may well see virginity as an eschatological value, as well as using it as a metaphor for fidelity and constancy. They are totally dedicated to the Lamb (v. 41); they have not raised their voice in giving honor to the beast (v. 5).*

The Three Angels (vv. 6-13)

There is a basic symmetry to the harvest picture. The perfect number seven appears: three angels announce the end, three angels execute it, and the son of Man stands at the center. The first *angel announces judgment and indicates there is still time for repentance (vv. 6–7).* Good news (Gr.: euangelion): *Announcing the deliverance of the final times, drawn from Hebrew rather than Christian eschatology (Is 52:7). The* second *angel announces the fall of Rome, identified as Babylon, the biblical epitome of evil (Is 21:9; Jer 51:7–8; Dn 4:27), here the seat of Satanic world power (v. 8).* Drink the wine *(v. 8): To share in the sentiments of another. Idolatry and immorality were shared by Babylon (Rome) with the nations subject to it.*

The third *angel depicts the impending tragedy, now applying the wine image to God's anger (vv. 9–10). The verses are the source of John Steinbeck's celebrated novel,* The Grapes of Wrath. *These are the angry sentiments to be shared with those who practice emperor cult.* Burning sulfur *(v. 10): Reminiscent of the fate of Sodom and Gomorrah (Gn 19:24; Dt 29:23; Lk 17:29).* The fire that torments *(v. 11): Gehenna, a fiery pit outside Jerusalem, which in the intertestamental period became symbolic of eternal punishment. In the midst of this frightening outpouring of divine anger upon those who follow the beast, the holy ones are lifted up (v. 12). They have died in faith and good works; in death they are at peace (v. 13).*

The Harvest (vv. 14–20)

Christ appears again as the son of Man (Dn 7:13–14), bearing a crown (sovereignty) and wielding a sickle for the harvest (Jl 4:13–14; Mt 13:39). There is first a harvest of wheat, then one of grapes. The last three angels all proceed from the heavenly temple; they and the son of Man are involved in the final harvests. The wheat harvest (v. 16) quickly fades into the grape harvest (vv. 17–20). The wine press appears as the central image of God's wrath, with the trampling and crushing of the grapes symbolic of massive destruction. In exaggerated imagery, the blood of the grape pours out over the land to an exorbitant extent. It is the "grapes of wrath" at its most graphic, in a scene of vintage apocalyptic (Is 63:1–3). The imagery will continue in chapter 19. The destruction takes place outside the city (v. 20), thus preserving from harm the new Jerusalem and Zion, the dwelling place of the elect.

A TIME TO GATHER...

For many of us, the fall of the year was harvest time. So we have some point of identification with the end time imaged as a harvest in this chapter of Revelation. This season of the year, so often spoken of in terms of death, is also the harbinger of life. There is merriment and laughter as people glean the fields and harvest the grapes, a labor which leads to full silos and brimming wine presses as the grain and new vintage stave off winter's severity.

It is rather surprising that the Bible's last reference to the fruit of the vine is in a negative context. Wine becomes the blood of the grape with the presses overflowing as the end-time destruction prevails. Yet we should not be overly surprised, since the first mention of wine in the Bible is connected with Noah's vineyard, which leads to his drunkenness and his sons' debauchery (Gn 9). But in general wine is a symbol of goodness and divine favor. The apocalypse of Isaiah (cc. 24–27) has an end-time picture of cosmic destruction and salvation. The positive slant is presented in terms of a great banquet of excellent food and choice wines. In Proverbs, Wisdom invites the local citizenry to come and drink of her special vintage (c. 9). And, of course, it is over the third cup of the farewell meal that Jesus is presented in the synoptic gospels as pronouncing that greatest blessing, which we call the Eucharist. Yet in Revelation the wine turns bitter and is equated with death.

What could be more somber than the angels of death, the original "Grim Reapers," who extend their sickles to "harvest" the malefactors. It is a harvest without joy, the moment of tragic retribution, as accounts are settled in a final and definitive way. Technology today has modernized harvesting; it is much less a chore than in the past. But anyone who has known childhood on a farm has memories of that work and play on fall days that made of this an anticipated season.

Yet what a reversal all of this is! It is one of the sobering aspects of life that so many of its joys can suddenly become its sorrows. Parents watch their children grow and sacrifice much on their behalf. And at a given moment something goes very wrong; the lives of their offspring become the source of incredible pain as the children abandon the values their parents strove to impart. Or there may be the loss of a child, as a mother who gave that child life now stands at a graveside to bid her last farewell. It is a heartrending scene because it blends so much past joy with present sorrow. Or think of the sorrow connected with loving parents upon whom the ravages of age have been unleashed, and who are beginning a gradual decline. Again present sorrows become more acute because of past joys. Daily we face that jarring imagery of revelation wherein good and evil stand in juxtaposition, making both ends of the spectrum so striking.

"THOSE WHOSE WORKS FOLLOW THEM..."

"Blessed are the dead who die in the Lord." If there is one verse of this book that most people know, it is this one. In the midst of limitless catastrophe, the blessed are at rest. Their works follow them. Is the good we do quickly forgotten? Not in God's time. There is a lasting value to every ripple of good that is unleashed on the waters of life. God is as quick to acknowledge our goodness as he is to overlook our repented wrongdoing. What else does it mean for sin as red as scarlet to become as white as snow? We should never become so doubtful of God's forgiveness that we keep regurgitating past sins. Scrupulosity is the badge of the doubter, one who does not take seriously the clear teaching of the gospel. The person who is forgiven and forgets is a person of faith who takes God at his word; the past is past, and it is now time to move ahead. Sin is always tragic, and we would ardently love to distance ourselves from it at every turn. But the fact is that all too often we do not, and at given moments in our life we have sinned grievously. But as Paul says to the Romans, "Where sin increased, grace overflowed all the more" (5:20). Rather than dwell on the gravity of what has occurred, why do we not consider the greatness of God's love? It is in the realization of our weakness and God's goodness that our life will move ahead. The picture of God's wrath in Revelation is directed to the unrepentant, those who find no place for God or his forgiveness in life. The rejection of forgiveness or an insensitivity to its necessity is the great human tragedy, not the fact that we have failed.

For those who stand in the company of the Lamb there is only peace and joy. Their death is transitional, not terminal; they die in friendship with God, and the good they have done becomes part of the treasury of the kingdom. "I was hungry and you gave me to eat; I was thirsty and you gave me to drink; I was in prison and you visited me." The works of the good accompany them on their final journey and stand them in good stead before the Lord. Even that which is done privately, with no fanfare, is known to the Lord and is not forgotten. We do not do good in order to be repaid, either here or in eternity. We are not working our way to God. That would be the type of exertion that Paul tells the Romans is not consonant with Christianity. We only say that

God is not unmindful. Every time we extend ourselves to others, the world is enriched; goodness becomes more pervasive. Nothing is too small or insignificant. Whatever in our lives is an expression of faith, with love speaking of a salvation already present and being articulated, has to tell us that we are not stepping over stones to reach salvation. Anything in our life that springs from the Spirit simply incarnates the reign of God to an ever greater degree. Goodness bridges the gap between here and eternity. "For their works accompany them." It is the only baggage we carry, and we will never feel the weight.

Yes, the chapter presents a picture of startling contrasts. The circling angels with their woeful plaint, the reapers on their mission of death, the overflowing winepress all speak of the demise of a world too well known. But then there is the Lamb and his exalted retinue, the harpists and the choir, those who have kept "God's commandments and their faith in Jesus." It includes the great saints and martyrs of the ages but also all those countless people who struggled from day to day and did their best at doing good. It is encouraging to know that there is light at the end of the tunnel and that nothing is ever really lost.

Thinking about the Harvest...

1. In Revelation, there is terror in God's judgment. How do you view this today?

2 What in today's world would be like "the virgins who follow the Lamb"?

3. How do you view music and song as part of the weekly liturgy?

4. In Revelation, what is the relationship between faith and works?

5. How do you understand hell?

6. We often speak of the "Grim Reaper." Does he adequately express your view of death?

7. What is the relevance of John Steinbeck's *The Grapes of Wrath* to the Book of Revelation?

THE SEVEN LAST PLAGUES (15:1–16:21)

15:1 Then I saw in heaven another sign, great and awe-inspiring: seven angels with the seven last plagues, for through them God's fury is accomplished.

15:2 Then I saw something like a sea of glass mingled with fire. On the sea of glass were standing those who had won the victory over the beast and its image and the number that signified its name. They were holding God's harps,

15:3 and they sang the song of Moses, the servant of God,
and the song of the Lamb:
"Great and wonderful are your works,
    Lord God almighty.
Just and true are your ways,
    O king of the nations.

15:4 Who will not fear you, Lord,
    or glorify your name?
For you alone are holy.
    All the nations will come
    and worship before you,
    for your righteous acts have been revealed."

15:5 After this I had another vision. The temple that is the heavenly tent of testimony opened,

15:6 and the seven angels with the seven plagues came out of the temple. They were dressed in clean white linen, with a gold sash around their chests.

15:7 One of the four living creatures gave the seven angels seven gold bowls filled with the fury of God, who lives forever and ever.

15:8 Then the temple became so filled with the smoke from God's glory and might that no one could enter it until the seven plagues of the seven angels had been accomplished.

THE SEVEN BOWLS

16:1 I heard a loud voice speaking from the temple to the seven angels, "Go and pour out the seven bowls of God's fury upon the earth."

16:2 The first angel went and poured out his bowl on the earth. Festering and ugly sores broke out on those who had the mark of the beast or worshiped its image.

16:3 The second angel poured out his bowl on the sea. The sea turned to blood like that from a corpse; every creature living in the sea died.

16:4 The third angel poured out his bowl on the rivers and springs of water. These also turned to blood.

16:5 Then I heard the angel in charge of the waters say:
"You are just, O Holy One,
   who are and who were,
   in passing this sentence.

16:6 For they have shed the blood of the holy ones and the
   prophets,
   and you [have] given them blood to drink;
   it is what they deserve."

16:7 Then I heard the altar cry out,
   "Yes, Lord God almighty,
   your judgments are true and just."

16:8 The fourth angel poured out his bowl on the sun. It was given the power to burn people with fire.

16:9 People were burned by the scorching heat and blasphemed the name of God who had power over these plagues, but they did not repent or give him glory.

16:10 The fifth angel poured out his bowl on the throne of the beast. Its kingdom was plunged into darkness, and people bit their tongues in pain

16:11 and blasphemed the God of heaven because of their pains and sores. But they did not repent of their works.

16:12 The sixth angel emptied his bowl on the great river Euphrates. Its water was dried up to prepare the way for the kings of the East.

16:13 I saw three unclean spirits like frogs come from the mouth of the dragon, from the mouth of the beast, and from the mouth of the false prophet.

16:14 These were demonic spirits who performed signs. They went out to the kings of the whole world to assemble them for the battle on the great day of God the almighty.

16:15 ("Behold, I am coming like a thief." Blessed is the one who watches and keeps his clothes ready, so that he may not go naked and people see him exposed.)

16:16 They then assembled the kings in the place that is named Armageddon in Hebrew.

16:17 The seventh angel poured out his bowl into the air. A loud voice came out of the temple from the throne, saying, "It is done."

16:18 Then there were lightning flashes, rumblings, and peals of thunder, and a great earthquake. It was such a violent earthquake that there has never been one like it since the human race began on earth.

16:19 The great city was split into three parts, and the gentile cities fell. But God remembered great Babylon, giving it the cup filled with the wine of his fury and wrath.

16:20 Every island fled, and mountains disappeared.

16:21 Large hailstones like huge weights came down from the sky on people, and they blasphemed God for the plague of hail because this plague was so severe.

This is the last series of plagues, following upon the seven seals and the seven trumpets. By this time, the reader hopes, we have finally come to the end. With a little patience the answer is positive. These plagues herald the end.

The operative texts: The plagues (Ex 7–12); the Song of Moses (Ex 15).

Chapter 15 begins by pointing to destruction as imminent. Again one must keep in mind that this is another replay of the same notion of judgment in the concentric circles to which we have become accustomed. Here the seven last plagues are introduced consecutively. But once again it is the "saved" who come to the fore. Sea of glass *(v. 2): This is a transparent sea, as the waters above the heavens were believed to be. The elect have not worshiped the emperor (beast, image, and number 666). They hold their harps and are presented as singing the great song of deliverance, the Song of Moses (Ex 15). Although the hymn does not borrow explicitly from the Song of Moses, it draws on a number of hymns, forming an Old Testament collage drawn from different sources (Ps 92:8; 98:1; Dt 32:4). But the image is clear enough: the deliverance of the elect is mirrored in the events of the exodus, as they pass through the waters of victory. The fire symbolizes the purifying ordeals through which the elect have had to pass in reaching their moment of triumph.*

The Exodus hymn gloried in the defeat of the enemy. This hymn (vv. 3–4) does not; it centers wholly on the glory of God. The victory song is central in the midst of all the tribulation that ensues, a victory that is not yet achieved but is real. The song lifts up the past (the exodus), the present (the glory of God) and the future (the assurance of deliverance), much the same as our liturgy does today.

With the appearance of the seven angels bearing the seven bowls, the final scene of catastrophe is about to begin. We have already witnessed the chaos inflicted in the scenes of the seven seals and the seven trumpets. Once again the Exodus plagues serve as the backdrop.

A solemn procession inaugurates the scene as the angels proceed from the temple (vv. 5–8). Tent of testimony *(v. 5): Here the temple merges with the Exodus meeting tent of the desert. This helps to preserve the Exodus character of the chapter (Ex 25:9,40) and points up Yahweh as the source of the final plagues. The angels are dressed in* priestly *robes and* royal *sashes (1:13; Ex 28:4). The bowls are filled with God's wrath, that is, his sentiments of anger which are now to be shared with the sinful population. The smoke-filled temple is inaccessible until the punishment is complete. The moment is intensely dramatic as the seven angels hold their bowls poised to let their contents descend on the earth.*

The seven bowls have striking parallels with the Egyptian plagues:

- *Sores (16:2) and the sixth plague (Ex 9:8–12)*

- *Bloody waters (16:3–4) and the fifth plague (Ex 7:17–21)*

- *Darkness (16:10) and the ninth plague (Ex 10:21–23)*

- *Frogs (16:13) and the second plague (Ex 8:25–29)*

    • *Thunder, fire, hail (16:18–21) and the seventh plague (Ex 9:13–26).*

    The dry river bed (16:12), in Exodus an avenue of deliverance (14:21–22), here enables the arrival of the destroying forces.

    As dreadful as these final plagues are, they are meant to illustrate the extent to which evil exists and the impossibility of its coexisting with God. It is explained in terms of the justice of God in defense of the persecuted in the hymn after the third bowl (16:5–6). From the divine perspective, as John sees it, the evil that has been perpetrated cannot be overlooked.

    An interesting historical note appears in this end-time conflict. A move against Rome comes in the form of invading Parthians (the kings of the East) from a point beyond the Euphrates (16:12–14). With the dried-up river they are provided easy access in their move against the beast. With battle lines now drawn, the kings of the earth are inspired by evil spirits to gather for final warfare (16:14–16). Armageddon *(16:16): "The mountain of Megiddo." This is where King Josiah died (2 Chr 35:2–24) and other battles and historic events took place (Jgs 5:19–20; 2 Kgs 9:27). As symbolic of the final battle it takes on end-time significance. A final admonition to vigilance is given by God (16:15; 3:3; Mt 24:42–44).*

    At this point the seventh angel ushers in the final cataclysm, to be spelled out in greater details in chapters 17–18. Like the end of Valhalla, symbolic Rome falls in the midst of overwhelming cosmic upheaval. And ironically, the blasphemies of the wicked persist to the very end (16:17–21).

THE SEA OF GLASS

Only a creative surrealist could capture the impact of the seven bowls, with their striking contrasts of deliverance and destruction. The elect of God stand on water that is as smooth as glass and sing the praises of God in Exodus-like tones. Almost simultaneously the seven angels of destruction are poised with the containers of God's fury, ready to pour it on the heads of agents of evil.

    Water is a recurrent biblical theme. It is both a source of life and a source of destruction. Just as the parting of the Red Sea meant deliverance at one point, so in Revelation the dry bed of the Euphrates spells invasion. The Genesis flood kills the wayward but provides for the safety of Noah, who is saved "from the waters," just as the Israelites are saved "through the waters." At the Red Sea the waters parted, and the Hebrews made their passage dry shod. They then sing their hymn of thanks for God's saving action on their behalf. A similar hymn is sung by the elect in Revelation as they stand upon the "sea of glass."

Between these two poles of biblical salvation, the beginning and the end, stands Christian baptism, so central to the life of all of us who bear the name "Christian." It is for us a death and resurrection effected by the power of God, a salvation "through the waters." Its significance is to be lived out daily, a dying to self and all its "fleshlike" death dealing concerns and a rising to a new life in God. And it is intended to make all the difference in the world. The song of victory only makes sense when victory is assured, and it occurs when God's mighty power is experienced. The truth is that death is vanquished and evil overcome no less in baptism than in any of the great saving acts of God and the Lamb. How important it is for the baptized to grasp that truth! It is easy to understand why adult baptism was so much the custom in the early church; then the sense of commitment could be deeply felt. The liturgical renewal has given the sacrament a preeminence and has highlighted its striking symbolism—water, candle, oil, vesture. But all of that which is symbol is meant to be brought to life.

And yet how easily baptism can be trivialized. Its social significance often seems to outweigh its meaning as the foundation of the Christian life. What it really means is sharing a new life with Christ as our brother, a real incorporation into the family of God. It means a call and an empowerment to live as "light" and "salt" in a problematic world where Christ desires to make a difference. It means living new values that spell true happiness but do not come cheaply. Sometimes baptism is evidently being carried out because it is the thing to do. Or it is an opportunity to bring friends and family together. And since restaurants are often harder to book than churches, the interests of the former take precedence over the latter. Godparents are chosen for a variety of reasons, and the quality of their Christian life is not always high on the list. A good catechesis of baptism is vitally important if the flame of faith is to be kept alive.

A LIFE COMMITMENT

For those of us who stand on the "sea of glass," formation in the faith becomes paramount. It means learning to pray and to live in an upright fashion. In the case of a child, as the learning process begins and develops, the meaning of our belief in God and the Son whom he sent is imparted. As the time comes for first Eucharist and Reconciliation, the family becomes the first educator. Nothing teaches like lived example. If these sacraments are meaningful to parents, there is good reason to believe they will be the same to the children. The flame of faith is tried during the difficult teens, when once again example says so much more than words. In short, our journey through the Red Sea can be long and tortuous, as we move toward that desert engagement with God to which we are all called. But it is precisely that—a journey—to which we are called, and not a park bench on the highway of life. Baptism was never meant as a magic formula that assures salvation. Rather it meant setting off on a new path with a new vision, which has to be constantly focused and made central to our lives.

By the same token, as we pursue the challenge of our baptismal commitment, it would be incorrect to think that such a vision and its internal Spirit can be easily lost. It is certainly possible to turn one's back on God and walk another path. And to turn away from God in deliberate and serious ingratitude can only be termed serious sin. But it just doesn't happen that simply. The truth of the matter is that our life in God is determined much more by the orientation and overall direction of our life than by single acts which cause us to stumble and fall. We have perhaps spent too much time on the notion of falling in and out of mortal sin, the sometimes frequent loss and recovery of the Spirit life within us. It is a concept that Saint Paul would find baffling, to say the least. It may not be always easy to decide. But if mortal sin is so lethal and death dealing, then it cannot be as frequent and common as we often have thought. And that is not to say that it does not exist or that there are not circumstances where a single act can be death-producing. But it is also true that our moral stance and posture are primarily determined not by what happened yesterday but by the general tenor of our life. The major moral question to be asked always and answered in truth is this: Is my life guided by moral principle and the direction of the Spirit, or are the demands of the "flesh," that is, my sinful inclinations more important? A single mishap on the journey does not always spell the journey's end. Just as a passive and morally insensitive pathway or a spiritual indifference does not mean that the journey is still in progress. These are important questions that do not always admit ready answers. But they merit weighty consideration.

THE SERIOUSNESS OF SIN

The angels' bowls pour forth God's punishment in ways reminiscent of the Egyptian plagues. The note of devastation is powerful—for some people, revolting and unworthy of God. But it has one purpose only: to underscore the seriousness of sin. We probably find the imagery jarring and more suited to an earlier millennium than our own. We have come to know God's Son, who for all intents and purposes had another agenda, not that of "fire and brimstone." But something else is involved here. We have also become anesthetized to sin. Sin can go quite unrecognized today because of its attractive guises. It is relativized, minimized, and sidetracked whenever possible. If at one time we made far too much of sin, the question now is how much attention do we give it at all. Former taboos in media and entertainment are today considered dated and out of place. The general breakdown of values in our society is today widely recognized and seldom addressed. Revelation is a healthy antidote in calling sin by name. Sin is the ultimate hostility toward God and therefore is painted in the darkest possible hues. It also has to meet its end. The end-time battle will not end in a tie; there is no trade-off. "All the nations will come and worship before you, for your righteous acts have been revealed" (15:4). There is only one Lord, and his dominion is total. We need not press the imagery of Revelation, but its basic truth is incontrovertible.

Thus, between the Red Sea and the sea of glass stand all of us who have been saved "through the waters." Can we not make a difference? Can we keep our vision clear?

God and the Presence of Evil in Our Lives

1. Every Sunday liturgy unites us with the past, present, and future. How is this so?

2. God is present in different sites: the temple, the tent, and the altar. Can you identify other sites?

3. In your own life, how is the presence of God felt? The presence of the beast?

4. What does it mean to experience "the cup of God's wrath"?

5. The image of the thief in the night urges us to be spiritually prepared. Do we take it seriously?

6. The Armageddon is the final battle. Is it not already in progress? In what sense?

7. Babylon, the great harlot, has had different applications in history. Do you know of any instances?

THE PUNISHMENT OF BABYLON AND THE DESTRUCTION OF PAGAN NATIONS

BABYLON THE GREAT (17:1–18)

17:1 **Then one of the seven angels who were holding the seven bowls came and said to me, "Come here. I will show you the judgment on the great harlot who lives near the many waters.**

17:2 **The kings of the earth have had intercourse with her, and the inhabitants of the earth became drunk on the wine of her harlotry."**

17:3 Then he carried me away in spirit to a deserted place where I saw a woman seated on a scarlet beast that was covered with blasphemous names, with seven heads and ten horns.

17:4 The woman was wearing purple and scarlet and adorned with gold, precious stones, and pearls. She held in her hand a gold cup that was filled with the abominable and sordid deeds of her harlotry.

17:5 On her forehead was written a name, which is a mystery, "Babylon the great, the mother of harlots and of the abominations of the earth."

17:6 I saw that the woman was drunk on the blood of the holy ones and on the blood of the witnesses to Jesus.
When I saw her I was greatly amazed.

17:7 The angel said to me, "Why are you amazed? I will explain to you the mystery of the woman and of the beast that carries her, the beast with the seven heads and the ten horns.

17:8 The beast that you saw existed once but now exists no longer. It will come up from the abyss and is headed for destruction. The inhabitants of the earth whose names have not been written in the book of life from the foundation of the world shall be amazed when they see the beast, because it existed once but exists no longer, and yet it will come again.

17:9 Here is a clue for one who has wisdom. The seven heads represent seven hills upon which the woman sits. They also represent seven kings:

17:10 five have already fallen, one still lives, and the last has not yet come, and when he comes he must remain only a short while.

17:11 The beast that existed once but exists no longer is an eighth king, but really belongs to the seven and is headed for destruction.

17:12 The ten horns that you saw represent ten kings who have not yet been crowned; they will receive royal authority along with the beast for one hour.

17:13 They are of one mind and will give their power and authority to the beast.

17:14 They will fight with the Lamb, but the Lamb will conquer them, for he is Lord of lords and king of kings, and those with him are called, chosen, and faithful."

17:15 Then he said to me, "The waters that you saw where the harlot lives represent large numbers of peoples, nations, and tongues.

17:16 The ten horns that you saw and the beast will hate the harlot; they will leave her desolate and naked; they will eat her flesh and consume her with fire.

17:17 For God has put it into their minds to carry out his purpose and to make them come to an agreement to give their kingdom to the beast until the words of God are accomplished.

17:18 The woman whom you saw represents the great city that has sovereignty over the kings of the earth."

THE FALL OF BABYLON (18:1–24)

18:1 After this I saw another angel coming down from heaven, having great authority, and the earth became illumined by his splendor.

18:2 He cried out in a mighty voice:
"Fallen, fallen is Babylon the great.
   She has become a haunt for demons.
She is a cage for every unclean spirit,
   a cage for every unclean bird,
   [a cage for every unclean] and disgusting [beast].

18:3 For all the nations have drunk
   the wine of her licentious passion.
The kings of the earth had intercourse with her,
   and the merchants of the earth grew rich from her drive for
   luxury."

18:4 Then I heard another voice from heaven say:
"Depart from her, my people,

so as not to take part in her sins
and receive a share in her plagues,

18:5 for her sins are piled up to the sky,
and God remembers her crimes.

18:6 Pay her back as she has paid others.
Pay her back double for her deeds.
Into her cup pour double what she poured.

18:7 To the measure of her boasting and wantonness
repay her in torment and grief;
for she said to herself,
'I sit enthroned as queen;
I am no widow,
and I will never know grief.'

18:8 Therefore, her plagues will come in one day,
pestilence, grief, and famine;
she will be consumed by fire.
For mighty is the Lord God who judges her."

18:9 The kings of the earth who had intercourse with her in their wantonness will weep and mourn over her when they see the smoke of her pyre.

18:10 They will keep their distance for fear of the torment inflicted on her, and they will say:
"Alas, alas, great city,
Babylon, mighty city.
In one hour your judgment has come."

18:11 The merchants of the earth will weep and mourn for her, because there will be no more markets for their cargo:

18:12 their cargo of gold, silver, precious stones, and pearls; fine linen, purple silk, and scarlet cloth; fragrant wood of every kind, all articles of ivory and all articles of the most expensive wood, bronze, iron, and marble;

18:13 cinnamon, spice, incense, myrrh, and frankincense; wine, olive oil, fine flour, and wheat; cattle and sheep, horses and chariots, and slaves, that is, human beings.

18:14 "The fruit you craved
   has left you.
All your luxury and splendor are gone,
   never again will one find them."

18:15 The merchants who deal in these goods, who grew rich
from her, will keep their distance for fear of the torment
inflicted on her. Weeping and mourning,

18:16 they cry out:
"Alas, alas, great city,
   wearing fine linen, purple and scarlet,
   adorned [in] gold, precious stones, and pearls.

18:17 In one hour this great wealth has been ruined."
Every captain of a ship, every traveler at sea, sailors, and
seafaring merchants stood at a distance

18:18 and cried out when they saw the smoke of her pyre, "What
city could compare with the great city?"

18:19 They threw dust on their heads and cried out, weeping
and mourning:
"Alas, alas, great city,
   in which all who had ships at sea
   grew rich from her wealth.
In one hour she has been ruined.

18:20 Rejoice over her, heaven,
   you holy ones, apostles, and prophets.
For God has judged your case against her."

18:21 A mighty angel picked up a stone like a huge millstone
and threw it into the sea and said:
"With such force will Babylon the great city be thrown down,
   and will never be found again.

18:22 No melodies of harpists and musicians,
   flutists and trumpeters,
   will ever be heard in you again.
No craftsmen in any trade
   will ever be found in you again.

**No sound of the millstone
  will ever be heard in you again.**

18:23 **No light from a lamp
  will ever be seen in you again.
No voices of bride and groom
  will ever be heard in you again.
Because your merchants were the great ones of the world,
  all nations were led astray by your magic potion.**

18:24 **In her was found the blood of prophets and holy ones
  and all who have been slain on the earth."**

It is one of the bowl angels (v. 1) who connects the events described in chapter 17 with those of the preceding chapter. This is another superimposed image heralding the inevitable denouement: *the crushing of the evil power. Interestingly enough, here we have both the image (vv. 1–6) and its interpretation (vv. 7–18).*

The harlot *(vv. 1, 18): This is the city of evil, Rome, called Babylon, here presented as a prostitute. Cities imaged as women are not unusual—thus virgin Jerusalem (Is 37:22, Lam 2:13), faithful wife and mother (Is 66:7–14), or unfaithful wife (Ez 16). Nineveh and Tyre are harlots (Na 3:1–7; Is 23).* Many waters *(v. 1): Babylon, rather than Rome, stood at the confluence of different waterways. Her sexual relations with the kings refers to Rome's idolatrous and godless practices in leading royalty and nations astray. She is the epitome of wanton godlessness in leading people from the truth. She is seated on the beast, as images converge here, with the latter also symbolizing Rome.* Blasphemous names *(v. 3): Profanations of God (13:5). The red beast carries the color of lasciviousness and promiscuity, just as white is the symbol of innocence.* Seven heads *(v. 3): The seven hills of Rome and the seven emperors of Rome. Her jewelry is the symbol of her wealth, and the cup holds the drink of her idolatrous conduct (v. 4). She is already drunk on the blood of the innocent she has killed (v. 6). Her title (v. 5) is perhaps the most derogatory in all of the Bible, and aptly identifies the whole scene as nothing but appalling. All of this points to the extent to which persecution had marked the life of the early Christians, who stand behind this imagery.*

Explanation of the Mystery (vv. 7–18)

The beast that once existed, exists no more, and will exist again (v. 8) refers to Nero redivivus, whose return from death was predicted. The seven kings (v. 9) are difficult to identify historically. The eighth is clearly Nero returned (v. 11). The seven may well signify simply the full complement of Caesars, that is, a round number. The ten horns (v. 12) seemingly represent kings who had been Roman sovereigns.

This confluence of evil power will persecute the Lamb (in his followers) but will not overcome (v. 14). Lord of lords and king of kings *(v. 14): Titles often given to the emperor but appropriate only when applied to Christ. The beast turns on the harlot (v. 16), pointing to a divided kingdom that crumbles from within. It is a disintegration of allegiance that has been directed by God himself (v. 17).*

The Chants of Destruction (c. 18)

This is a collage of biblical texts with a remarkable variety of images and actions pointing to the final immolation of Babylon, the great evil.

They echo various chants over destroyed cities and countries (Is 13;23;34; 47; Jer 50;51; Zep 2).

The first voice (vv. 1–3): *Sins and sanctions are to the fore. Desolation and destruction are the lot of the fallen Babylon in light of the sins of passion, fornication, and luxury, which translate into idolatry and godlessness.*

The second voice (vv. 4–8): *The elect are encouraged to take their leave of the great evil, in a moral not a literal sense, that is, separation from her sinful ways. The contrast is worth noting. She boasted of being the queen of the lot, with no grief or mourning of any type, but she is now to be repaid with plagues, famine, and grief. But it is all to be seen as the judgment of God on history and human conduct (v. 8). God's triumph over evil is inevitable and inexorable. Then her former lovers stand at a distance and grieve over her funeral pyre, watching this rapid and decisive demise (vv. 9–10).*

The merchants of international trade (vv. 11–17): *They have lost their best market. Their goods range from precious stones and jewels and household objects to foodstuffs, livestock, and even slaves. They too chant the loss of all that was precious.*

The sailors (vv. 19–20) *stand at a distance also. The funeral pyre is of such size and intense heat that it does not permit any closeness. There is rejoicing (v. 20) mixed with grief as the heavenly company sees God's judgment being executed.*

The mighty angel (vv. 21–24) *casts the sinking stone, symbolic of total loss, evocative of Jeremiah's prophecy (51:63–64; cf. Mk 9:42). In the song we get a glimpse of the one-time glory that was Rome with its music (v. 22a), artisans (v. 22b), light and happiness (v. 23a), and trade and commerce (v. 23b). Yet they were all overshadowed by her evil-doing (v. 24).*

PROSTITUTING OR SAVING LIFE

Prostitution as a metaphor for idolatry is not uncommon in the scriptures, but it has no more graphic expression than in the Book of Revelation. Seated on a scarlet beast, the harlot wears purple and scarlet and is festooned with a variety of jewelry. She has cavorted with numerous kings and people of power. She is called "Babylon" because the Jews never had a more formidable (or hated) foe; it was in that city that they had sat and wept in exile as they remembered Zion (Ps 137). In the present first-century context of Revelation, the prostitute is Rome and the beast on which she rides represents the emperors who had directed the empire over the years. She has made her fortune through dealings with foreign kings, and she has become a center of international trade. On these foreigners she is said to have showered her sexual favors, seeing herself as invincible and desired by all. Now that the final reckoning has come, her end is in sight.

From any perspective, be it biblical, Christian, or secular, the great harlot has appeared repeatedly in history. And her demise has been presided over an equal number of times. From one point of view, an "evil empire" is one that is godless, repressive, and absolute in its claims. When it collapses, the event seems to have eschatological significance, with the power of "good" triumphing over "evil." But the imagery cannot be pressed too far, because the overcoming force or the power that shows greater endurance cannot easily be equated with the avenging angel. The fact is that there are many ways, some of them quite subtle, by which people may be dominated or "prostituted," and which may not entail a wholesale repression or domination. Some of the forces that win in history are no less godless than those that they vanquish.

As a result, the many ways the woman and the beast have been identified in the course of history have proven to be quite simplistic. A long view of history reminds us that Rome as the center of Catholicism has been characterized as a female seductress in the minds of those who held the Catholic Church in little favor, even up until modern times. While it may well be reasonable to take consolation from the fact that, within the twentieth century, massive forces of evil have not endured, it would be wrong to interpret this theologically in terms of the power of good over evil. It is possible to meditate with profit on the evil expansion of the Nazi dream and the death and destruction that came in its wake without canonizing the victor. The empire destined to last one thousand years did not survive, but its end did not usher in the final age. There is, moreover, no single factor that explains the end of the Soviet empire, but the fact remains that in its ruthless and godless aims it did not survive. But only unthinking politicians or equally inept evangelizers are quick to establish the battle lines of the Armageddon in determining the "we" and the "they." We have not yet reached the moment where any political system can claim to be sufficiently selfless and people-centered so as to be free of any taint of the beast.

FAITH AND CITY LIFE

Cities play an interesting role in the unfolding of the biblical plan. Babylon is symbolic of the evil connected with the center of an empire. It was the seat of an emperor and a major metropolitan center. It was from there, deep in ancient Mesopotamia, that the giant tentacles of an expansionist regime finally reached the shores of the Mediterranean. It was there, in this seat of an ancient culture, that the exiled Israelites lamented their inability to sing a song of the Lord in a foreign land (Ps 137). Here a people for whom the temple and the land signified the very presence of God were forced to come to a new dimension of faith, a faith without those concrete supports. Eventually Jeremiah will exhort the exiled people to settle, build houses, plant gardens, and marry. They are to promote the well-being of the city and even pray for it (Jer 29).

The stay in Babylon was an experience of metropolitan life for which the Israelites were unprepared. And yet it was then that their understanding of God expanded. They became more inclusive, less linked to geography and a localized deity, and thus became better prepared to become the post–exilic "People of the Book." This is to say that city life in the scriptures cannot simply be equated with sin. As a melting pot of peoples and ideas, the city can become a catalyst in the process of ongoing revelation.

At one point even the mention of Nineveh could stir negative feelings in the heart of an Israelite believer. It was the first major threat to Israel's security, and it succeeded in destroying and deporting a large part of the northern kingdom. The Assyrians were ruthless invaders, and it was to their capital Nineveh that they brought their captives and the spoils of their conquest. And yet in the parable that makes up the Book of Jonah, it is to the Ninevites that the reluctant prophet is sent. As he walks through the vast city he proclaims the need for repentance and forgiveness. And the people capitulate in incredible numbers! Granting that the book is not meant to be historical, the fact remains that its call for a more inclusive sense of God's concern is located in one of the most unlikely, indeed inimical sites in the Old Testament.

City life has not always treated the Hebrews well. In Egypt's royal cities of Pithom and Raamses, there were few bright memories for a people counted as slave labor. It was from there that they were delivered and led into the desert, where communication with God was facilitated. But city life took another turn for the better when Canaan was reached and David, with keen political acumen, captured the Jebusite city of Jerusalem and established it as a seat of government and faith. It is around this city that the bulk of Israelite history revolves. Thus, it is not totally accurate to think of the desert as the only idyll of Hebrew religious thought, as the single place of solitude and communion with God, as if it were something of a forerunner to the coenobitic and heremitical mentality of *fuga mundi*. As much if not more happens in the cities to advance biblical thought than in privileged isolation.

CITIES AND CHRISTIANITY

In the earliest Christian times, it is again Jerusalem that remains pivotal. The synoptic gospels have Jesus visit it only once in the course of his public ministry (which lasts less than a year), whereas John has him make three pilgrimages to the holy city. But it is always to Jerusalem that the eyes of Jesus turn. In Luke's Gospel, the journey of Jesus to Jerusalem begins in the ninth chapter. As he makes his way to the city apart from which no prophet can die, he unfolds his teaching for the benefit of his disciples. Once Jesus reaches Jerusalem, he never again departs. For Luke, in that city the redemptive act of Jesus transpires, and it is there that the Spirit invests the disciples for their mission to the world. These religious and theological events of human history invest the city of Jerusalem with unparalleled importance.

It was in the Syrian city of Antioch that we were first called Christians (Acts 11:26), and in Athens that Paul made his celebrated appeal for conversion in a not overly successful attempt at hellenistic inculturation. He brought his missionary life to a conclusion in Rome. From this center of the empire, Christianity launched its beginning as a world religion.

Thus, while there are reasons why pagan Rome, as an early center of opposition to the church, can be labeled a woman of easy virtue astride her ugly beast, it cannot be denied that Rome also became historically a pivotal center for the effusion of God's truth. Moreover, it is the city of Jerusalem, beset by so many negatives in its long history, that is the heavenly city of the saved at the end of Revelation. While there is certainly a quality of life, peace, and serenity connected with the countryside, the world's population today, in ever increasing numbers, is finding its way to the city. And with all their problems, cities can be seen as blessed places where great holiness of life is to be found. We have our homeless and our agencies that strive to meet their needs. We have our hungry and our bread lines that daily try to provide sustenance. We have unemployment and human resources and agencies that work to overcome it. We have dedicated people of all faiths, or none, who work to change oppressive structures in addressing systemic evils. We hear the voice of conscience from those who are convinced that environmental concerns are both urgent and God-related. Above all, there are the prayers that rise from countless places of worship, separated by only a few blocks, in a day-long litany of praise. For all its noise and confusion, a city represents life, a strong pulse, a limitless creativity and energy. It is blessed with mind and spirit and a technology that can help to build the city of God. Its shadow side, assuredly, allies it with the great whore in greed and promiscuity, and in the idolatry of material wealth. But with it all, such a concentration of people, some believers, some nonbelievers, spells an unlimited power for good that must be factored into any consideration of spiritual empowerment.

It is sufficient to note that the image of sin presented as a seducing woman is matched by biblical descriptions of urban life in terms of spouse, wife, and mother.

FAITH AND INTERNATIONAL RELATIONS

"The kings of the earth will weep....The merchants of the earth will weep." Babylon, like Nineveh or Rome, was more than a city; it was the center of an empire. This meant diplomacy in interlocking state relationships, as well as commerce and trade. It is fascinating to see how these various pursuits touch on one another and are woven into the historical mix. Both trade and diplomacy are positive in themselves. Trade provides markets for goods, representing a gain for the buyer and the seller. Diplomatic contacts can cement ties between nations and prevent misguided steps that can trigger serious international consequences.

But just as milk may turn sour, that which is good can be misused and take devious turns. Larger nations may ally themselves with one another to the disadvantage of lesser states. Diplomacy may be used to produce vulnerability; it may become a destabilizing tool in making a country an easy victim. It may place ever more power in the hands of a few to the detriment of the majority. Diplomacy may be used to create blocks of power that present a threat to world peace. The intentions of the "kings and powers" may erode and diplomacy used as a tool to bolster the power of a leadership that holds little or no accountability to the majority. Some of the greatest conflicts of modern times came as a result of turning aside from the route of honest and praiseworthy diplomacy in favor of pacts in the interests of forming a united front against a threatening force. Faced by major "power plays," many smaller countries have simply been absorbed into the ambit of something larger than life, from which they were powerless to extricate themselves.

COMMERCE AND MORALITY

Trade is vitally important in politics and commerce, but its moral implications cannot be overlooked. Do we favor open markets or protectionism? Where does enlightened self-interest take precedence over the good of another? The argument continues to repeat itself. As soon as we open American markets to foreign goods, there will be a cry from some quarter that this is harmful to employment and will affect the job market adversely. But to close the door too forcefully on imports is bound to affect our exports as well. And that could be equally disastrous to jobs and the economy. To speak in general, and distinctly Christian terms, it is true to say that there should be free and open markets in the world today. Markets should not be the exclusive domain of any major power. Smaller countries have less diversified economies and therefore a greater need for opportunities that provide access to major markets. Unfortunately this is not always the case. The weak suffer at the hands of the strong, and those who already have want much more.

This ultimately leads to the question of capitalism, which is not an unmixed blessing. In the past it was so often contrasted with communism that there was a tendency to underscore its positive features and ignore its negatives. Its basic tenets, which uphold private property and free enterprise, are rooted in human dignity and therefore commendable in themselves. But greed rears its ugly head no less in corporate life than in individual morality. Ethical principles and a basic respect for others have to govern free enterprise if a sense of justice and equality is to prevail. It is the well-being of people—all people—that must regulate market forces. Profit cannot be the sole driving force without other important values being sacrificed on the altar of greed. When high-level merchandise is sold at handsome prices, yet manufactured in the sweatshops of Asia or Latin America, there is a serious violation of human rights and a sinful form of domination.

In Revelation, the merchants stand on their shores and weep as Babylon the great sinks into oblivion. The interlocking of interests could not be clearer. "No man is an island." Many suffer with the one. The opportunity once offered for mutual happiness has passed. Diplomacy and trade can carry us to different shores—for good or evil. It is a human choice.

FAITH AND THE FINE ARTS

"No melodies of harpists and musicians, flutists and trumpeters will ever be heard in you again." In the tragedy accompanying the end time, as presented in Revelation, there is the noted absence of music. Even though the description is more literary than literal, the beauty of music is clearly related to the presence of God, and its absence connotes dissonance and chaos. This brings to mind the realization of how much the fine arts add to the meaning of life. On a purely human level, music and art have the ability to lift or soothe our spirits and enable us to go beyond the terrestrial. For many people the arts are the great joy of their lives, and, if not a substitute for religion, the arts are certainly its complement. Music, for example, has the capacity to transcend the temporal and terrestrial and in some indefinable way reach out to the divine. It may be true that many of the world's greatest composers were not religious in the traditional sense, yet they themselves often recognized that their gifts were not easily explained.

It is not uncommon for a person to take leave of a concert hall enveloped in what may well be termed a "religious experience." In some instances it will say more of God than a church service. This is not mere hyperbole or emotional talk. There is a spark of the divine in much that artistic genius has contributed to the human scene over the centuries; biblical stories have served as the source of great painting, from da Vinci to Dali. Religious texts have been elevated to a new level of inspiration in musical compositions. Think of the "Requiem Aeternam" from Mozart's *Requiem* and the "Agnus Dei" of his *Coronation Mass*. The church, the great sponsor of the arts, has long seen their importance in contributing to religious experience. The artist is seen not as an accessory to faith but a vital communicator of its meaning. J. S. Bach, who was steeped in the Lutheran tradition, found that his faith so influenced his composing that it is said that he never wrote a page of secular music.

There is much in our life that is dissonant and disordered (and a fair amount of modern culture reflects it), yet harmony and the gift of the Muses enhance the human spirit. At their best, the fine arts point to the transcendent, going beyond the painting, the sculpture, the drama, the opera, or the symphony to a higher order where all of beauty converges. In a world that so often panders to the ungodly, we would be immensely impoverished without the arts. Every society should respect its artists and its cultural tradition. All education should hold it up as an expression of our noblest. In noting its absence, Revelation points to its value.

Reflections on Western Civilization

1. Do you think images are a useful way to express moral principles?

2. Rome, in Revelation, is the symbol of all evil. Yet in much of history it has been seen as a symbol of good. What is the distinction?

3. Discuss biblical cities that are seen in a positive light.

4. Do you see diplomacy as an instrument of peace? Does it also have a negative side?

5. Trade and commerce affect the lives of everyone for good or ill. How is this the case?

6. Why are the fine arts so important for humanity?

7. What are the dangers connected with big business?

8. In depicting evil today, what images would you use?

III. FINAL REDEMPTION AND THE NEW CREATION (19:1–22:5)

WEDDING FEAST AND ARMAGEDDON (19:1–21)

19:1 After this I heard what sounded like the loud voice of a great multitude in heaven, saying:
"Alleluia!
Salvation, glory, and might belong to our God,

19:2 for true and just are his judgments.
He has condemned the great harlot
   who corrupted the earth with her harlotry.
He has avenged on her the blood of his servants."

19:3 They said a second time:
"Alleluia! Smoke will rise from her forever and ever."

19:4 The twenty-four elders and the four living creatures fell down and worshiped God who sat on the throne, saying, "Amen. Alleluia."

THE VICTORY SONG
19:5 A voice coming from the throne said:
"Praise our God, all you his servants,
   [and] you who revere him, small and great."

19:6 Then I heard something like the sound of a great multitude or the sound of rushing water or mighty peals of thunder, as they said:
"Alleluia!

The Lord has established his reign,
[our] God, the almighty.

19:7 Let us rejoice and be glad
   and give him glory.
For the wedding day of the Lamb has come,
   his bride has made herself ready.

19:8 She was allowed to wear
   a bright, clean linen garment."
(The linen represents the righteous deeds of the holy ones.)

19:9 Then the angel said to me, "Write this: Blessed are those who have been called to the wedding feast of the Lamb." And he said to me, "These words are true; they come from God."

19:10 I fell at his feet to worship him. But he said to me, "Don't! I am a fellow servant of yours and of your brothers who bear witness to Jesus. Worship God. Witness to Jesus is the spirit of prophecy."

THE KING OF KINGS

19:11 Then I saw the heavens opened, and there was a white horse; its rider was [called] "Faithful and True." He judges and wages war in righteousness.

19:12 His eyes were [like] a fiery flame, and on his head were many diadems. He had a name inscribed that no one knows except himself.

19:13 He wore a cloak that had been dipped in blood, and his name was called the Word of God.

19:14 The armies of heaven followed him, mounted on white horses and wearing clean white linen.

19:15 Out of his mouth came a sharp sword to strike the nations. He will rule them with an iron rod, and he himself will tread out in the wine press the wine of the fury and wrath of God the almighty.

19:16 He has a name written on his cloak and on his thigh, "King of kings and Lord of lords."

19:17 Then I saw an angel standing on the sun. He cried out [in] a loud voice to all the birds flying high overhead, "Come here. Gather for God's great feast,

19:18 to eat the flesh of kings, the flesh of military officers, and the flesh of warriors, the flesh of horses and of their riders, and the flesh of all, free and slave, small and great."

19:19 Then I saw the beast and the kings of the earth and their armies gathered to fight against the one riding the horse and against his army.

19:20 The beast was caught and with it the false prophet who had performed in its sight the signs by which he led astray those who had accepted the mark of the beast and those who had worshiped its image. The two were thrown alive into the fiery pool burning with sulfur.

19:21 The rest were killed by the sword that came out of the mouth of the one riding the horse, and all the birds gorged themselves on their flesh.

This chapter, striking in its contrasts, joins the great nuptials (vv. 1–10) and the final pitched battle (vv. 11–21). This is the third panel of the triptych, as the seer is made privy to another series of seven events. Following upon the seven churches, seven seals, seven trumpets, and seven bowls, we now face climactically the seven final events. These are the Lamb's feast (19:1–10), the last battle (19:11–21), the binding of Satan (20:1–3), the millennium (20:4–7), the defeat of Gog and Magog (20:8–10), the last judgment (20:11–15), and the new Jerusalem (c. 21).

Some of the operative texts: Hosea 2:14–20; Isaiah 62:5; Jeremiah 2:2; Mark 2:19; John 3:29; 2 Corinthians 11:2; Ephesians 5:25–32; Matthew 22:1–14; 25:1–13.

The Final Chorus (vv. 1–8)

Among the participants are the great multitude (v. 1), which includes the elect and the saved of all nations (7:9–10). The full complement embraces the twenty-four elders and the four living creatures, who have

*been attendant at the throne throughout (v. 4). They are joined by a
"voice coming from the throne."*

After the intonation of the alleluia *("Praise Yahweh"), frequent in
the psalter, God is praised for crushing evil (the great harlot), who had
spread idolatry and killed witnesses to Christ (v. 2).* Smoke will rise
*(v. 3): Not the smoke of incense in praise of God but the putrid smoke of
a judgment executed on evil itself.*

*At this point there is an abrupt change, as the wedding day of the Lamb
and his bride is announced (v. 7). The latter is adorned in a bright linen
garment symbolic of the good deeds of the elect (v. 8; Mt 22:11–14). The
angel's speech (vv. 9–11) has echoes of Daniel (8:15–19), but may also be
a subtle polemic against the exaggerated exaltation of the angels in seg-
ments of the early church (Col 2:18; 2 Cor 11:14). Here the angel is
clearly subordinate to Christ.* Bear witness to Jesus *(v. 10): Here the
objective genitive is preferred. Any authentic prophecy looks to Jesus alone;
only he is "the Word of God" (v. 13), the perfect expression of divinity. All
martyrdom or prophecy is an expression of faith in him.*

The Vision of the Returning Warrior (vv. 11–16)

*This is a powerful but most unusual image of Christ. Seated on a white
horse, he is simply identified as "Faithful and True" (3:14; 1:5),
although his name is Word of God (v. 13: John 1:1). He is a fiery-eyed
warrior, crowned with jewels (1:14).* Cloak dipped in blood *(v. 13):
The blood shed by the Lamb for the salvation of others (7:14). Even in
the midst of vivid military imagery, it is the victory attained by Christ's
death that emerges.* The armies of heaven *(v. 12): The elect wearing
the white robes of salvation. Although the army is massive, it is Christ
alone who wages the war. The warrior rules "with an iron rod" (Ps 2:9),
wages a bloody war against the forces of evil, described in terms of
tramping the grapes in the wine press (v. 15; Is 63:3), and thus brings
about a full recognition of his kingship and lordship (v. 16).*

*With all the designation given the warrior king, he still retains an
unknown name (v. 12). Definitions give partial insight, but the
ultimate meaning of Christ remains mystery. Now we know partially
(1 Cor 13:9), "through a glass darkly"; fuller vision is reserved for
the future. Every name is a form of self-disclosure; the king still
retains a certain anonymity and a nameless sovereignty.*

The Vision of the Last Battle (vv. 17–21)

Here the two opposing forces face off in readiness for the final test. It is the horseman and his army of the elect against the evildoers of all classes, the kings of the earth, the beast, and the false prophet. There is no description of the battle, which, in fact, has already transpired in the death of the Lamb. The beast and the prophet are angrily consigned to a fiery abyss. Again the imagery is full of contrast: For the wedding feast of the Lamb (v. 9) is substituted a grisly vulture feast (v. 21), with bloody carnage in the bodies of the defeated evildoers. To both "feasts" invitations are extended (vv. 9,17).

THE MARRIAGE BOND

Contrasting images contribute powerfully to artistic and literary effectiveness. In Dante's *Divine Comedy,* there is the vividness present in the gradations of suffering in the Inferno offset by the glories of the Paradiso. Or on a visually powerful scale, there is the triumphant Christ and his retinue of the saved in Michelangelo's *Last Judgment* contrasted with the horrors of damnation visible in the faces of those who are perishing. So as Revelation moves rapidly toward its conclusion, we have the picture of Christ, the invincible horseman, ready for battle, which is coupled with the antecedent call to the Lamb's wedding feast, all to be followed by a pitched battle between the horseman and the beast with his minions. The final image is one of vultures devouring the wasted carnage. Perhaps nowhere in scripture is there a more graphic and penetrating presentation of human destiny in its choice of good or evil.

It is not surprising that the final deliverance of the just is depicted in terms of a wedding. It appears often enough in the prophets, where it images the definitive engagement of Yahweh and his people, and a violated marriage is used to illustrate the people's infidelity. In the New Testament the wedding becomes an eschatological symbol. The wedding feast inaugurated in the coming of Christ finds fasting inappropriate (Mk 2:18–22) and reminds the bridal party that a state of alertness in expectation of the groom's return is essential (Mt 25:1–12; 22:1–14). In human affairs the Jesus of the Gospels strenuously upholds the

permanence of the marriage bond and views the married state
in distinctly positive terms. In the epistolary literature, Ephesians
sees husband and wife as a mirror of the union between Christ
and his church (Eph 5:21–33).

And now the Bible closes with the same imagery. "The wedding day of the Lamb has come, his bride has made herself
ready." Marriage and end-time joy go hand in hand. The scriptures do not support a view that sees the rapture and pleasure
connected with the marriage commitment as tawdry or less than
worthy. If we are correct in our understanding of the Song of
Songs, we are reading a series of very tantalizing, even volup-
tuous love songs. And it should not be seen as at all strange.
What would be unusual would be a Hebrew view of the marriage
relationship as disjunctive; the physical and the spiritual are at
one in Hebrew thought as one body–person bonds with another.
It is only when the human person is viewed in hylomorphic
terms that an accompanying spirituality will see the soul as elevated and the body as less than worthy.

That our mortal nature is a weakened one is not in question. But
from the beginning it is as male and female that we are created.
Gender differences are inherent in the human condition and stand
at the very core of the marriage relationship. Hence, the physical
dimension of love is integral and therefore sacred, as well as an
image of the divine. To see it as less than human or even to speak of
the sexual relationship principally in terms of procreation is to
deprive it of its full meaning. It is intimacy that relates Christ to the
church and to every Christian, and the scriptures do not hesitate to
compare it to the deepest relationship between husband and wife.

COMMITMENT

Upon Christ, the fearless horseman, are bestowed three titles in
this chapter: Faithful and True, Word of God, and King of kings
and Lord of lords. They are not concepts new to Revelation, but
here they represent a summary of the book's Christology.
Covenant fidelity (Heb.: 'emeth) is one of the dominant and oft-
cited characteristics of Yahweh in the Old Testament. It is so
interwoven with the whole life and mission of Jesus that here,

appropriately, it is given to him as a name. The book opens (1:5) and here closes emphasizing the faithfulness of Jesus, his complete dedication to the mission entrusted to him.

For a variety of reasons the word *commitment* does not fall easily from our lips today. It seems that inevitably it is likely to hurt someone's feelings. If it is attached to something that is destined to last longer than a year, then it might be better to find another term! And yet how can we escape it, as commitment is so inextricably interwoven with the Christian vocation itself. Baptism is not a sometime sort of thing bound by time limitations. It is a lifelong pledge that we renew repeatedly as our life goes on. The Christian life means growth, a growing process no less real than our human and physical maturation. And yet we are constantly being met with the fact that people have "checked out" either on a temporary or permanent basis. But think of what that means. We cannot be Christians on our terms. If we carry his name, we live his values. And if Christ was anything, he was faithful and committed.

In so many areas of Christian life and vocation the word *commitment* has been relativized. Initial enthusiasm may wane, conflicting interests may intrude, or factors heretofore unknown begin to color our vision. Each case is different, and it is not for us to judge. In fact it is difficult to broach the subject because it has touched the lives of too many people whom we love dearly. But the effects are there for everyone to see. Without a sense of stability it is impossible for any segment of church or society to endure. To call divorce a major evil of our times is not to judge any individual person who has obtained one. It is simply to state a tragic fact. By the same token, we are stirred deeply when we meet a person who has proven to be "faithful and true." We know that it has not been a pain-free life and that there have been many crosses along the way. It is hard for a husband and wife to remain together when there have been deep hurts in the relationship. But many do persevere. When a priest sees his post-conciliar hopes for the church radically altered by unforeseen changes in the direction and mentality of ecclesiastical leadership, it is not easy to stay at the helm. The futuristic vision pales into gray conformity. It is a pain that has touched the lives of many. And yet they have not turned away but are often renewed in their dedication to what is paramount: the concerns of God's people. The cross has to be borne, and few of us are free of the burden. And yet what courage we take in seeing endurance written on the wizened faces of so many. The posture of their lives attests to their faith. It is a reflection of the Lord himself. Faithful and true.

NAMING GOD

Jesus is the Word of God at Revelation's end, much as he is at the beginning of John's Gospel. In fact it was with a word that God created in the first chapter of Genesis. God's word is an extension of himself; it is endowed with divine power. But a word is also an act of self-disclosure. It is by what we say that people know what is on our minds. An example might help. In the mid-1980s my mother suffered a stroke and lost her speech. She lived for four years in the midst of great frustration. She believed that she was communicating her thoughts, but it was actually nothing more than incoherent sounds. We had to guess what she was saying, and more often than not we were left without a clue. We suffered with her, but it taught me the value of words. When God creates with a word, he discloses much about himself. When he gives us his Son as his final Word, he tells us more than we could hope for.

The biblical word is dynamic, an extension of the speaker; it effects what it set out to do. A blessing or a curse once given is irrevocable; it takes on a life of its own. In a society which lived on words and not writing, the spoken word took on much more value than it does for us, whose words take to the winds and are quickly lost (forgotten). And so Jesus as the Word of God brings all of these ideas together. He is the final Word, the great act of self-disclosure, our "window on God." God is no longer simply an object of speculation. We now have a much clearer idea of who God is and what it is that makes him the God we worship. This is the God of the covenant, the God of outreach, care, and compassion, even to the point of self-donation. In what Jesus teaches, in his parables, in his miracles, in his conduct, but above all, in that example of divine love that is the Lamb who was slain, we come to an ever clearer idea of the God who is ours. As the Epistle to the Hebrews states, God spoke to us in many ways in times past, but in these final times he has spoken to us in his Son. And what would our life be if that Word were not spoken? Do we realize what a difference it makes? It is our whole life of faith. How often do we pick up God's Word and read? We can never be grateful enough. It is the Word which defines our life and under which we all stand in judgment.

It is probably easier for us to call Jesus "Lord" than "King." Kings are part neither of our life nor our vocabulary. We know them from history as either worthy leaders or despots. In a democratic society it is hard to imagine plenary power given to someone solely on the basis of dynastic tradition. Yet when we try to find an alternative title for Jesus we don't do much better. He is hardly a president, chairman of the board, or president of the trustees. But the idea is clear enough. Kingship means he holds the dominant sway over our lives. He is king because he won it, and he rules by persuasion. The horseman, remember, wears a cloak that has been dipped in blood. Christ comes to his kingship in the same way he became Lord, by offering himself as the Isaian servant of the Lord, the one who gave his life for many for the forgiveness of sins. It is, indeed, a different type of kingship.

All of this says very simply that it is to Jesus that we give the "obedience of faith." It is a reign to which we willingly submit because it is rooted in love and concern. It is an empire of willing citizens, a kingdom of dedicated and appreciative subjects. It is an important model. Authority exists for people, not vice versa. In church or society many of us are given authority; it may last for years or for a limited period of time. One of the great benefits of religious orders and congregations in the church is a limited period of service. Authority in most religious communities from the lowest to the highest (if you will excuse the limping imagery!) is for a fixed period of time. No one stays on for years on end, rescued only by retirement. As one witty superior stated it, "This illness is tolerable only because it is terminal." But what is most important is the lesson that Christ gives to anyone in authority. He asks for our allegiance in this as in everything else. His whole life was one of dedicated service. Control, domination, manipulation—all should be far from our thoughts. Inspiration, encouragement, recognition—let these be the hallmark of Christian office hold-ers. "Have this mind in you which was also in Christ Jesus...."

God's Word, then, is faithful and true, King of kings and Lord of lords. Revelation brings the whole meaning of Christ together in images that are new and sometimes startling. Behind all the imagery is a powerful message. It remains only for us to make it our own.

On Using Imagery

1. Is military imagery a suitable way to express a spiritual victory? Would you express it differently today?

2. Do you think that the wedding imagery aptly expresses our final union with God?

3. The importance of the name emerges continually in the Bible. Can you think of some examples?

4. What is the meaning of the "blood on the cloak"?

5. Although royalty is not a part of our culture, we continually give Christ royal titles. Do you have a problem with that?

THE MILLENNIUM: THE THOUSAND-YEAR REIGN (20:1–15)

20:1 Then I saw an angel come down from heaven, holding in his hand the key to the abyss and a heavy chain.

20:2 He seized the dragon, the ancient serpent, which is the Devil or Satan, and tied it up for a thousand years

20:3 and threw it into the abyss, which he locked over it and sealed, so that it could no longer lead the nations astray until the thousand years are completed. After this, it is to be released for a short time.

20:4 Then I saw thrones; those who sat on them were entrusted with judgment. I also saw the souls of those who had been beheaded for their witness to Jesus and for the word of God, and who had not worshiped the beast or its image nor had accepted its mark on their foreheads or hands. They came to life and they reigned with Christ for a thousand years.

20:5 The rest of the dead did not come to life until the thousand years were over. This is the first resurrection.

20:6 Blessed and holy is the one who shares in the first resurrection. The second death has no power over these; they will be priests of God and of Christ, and they will reign with him for [the] thousand years.

20:7 When the thousand years are completed, Satan will be released from his prison.

20:8 He will go out to deceive the nations at the four corners of the earth, Gog and Magog, to gather them for battle; their number is like the sand of the sea.

20:9 They invaded the breadth of the earth and surrounded the camp of the holy ones and the beloved city. But fire came down from heaven and consumed them.

20:10 The Devil who had led them astray was thrown into the pool of fire and sulfur, where the beast and the false prophet were. There they will be tormented day and night forever and ever.

THE LARGE WHITE THRONE

20:11 Next I saw a large white throne and the one who was sitting on it. The earth and the sky fled from his presence and there was no place for them.

20:12 I saw the dead, the great and the lowly, standing before the throne, and scrolls were opened. Then another scroll was opened, the book of life. The dead were judged according to their deeds, by what was written in the scrolls.

20:13 The sea gave up its dead; then Death and Hades gave up their dead. All the dead were judged according to their deeds.

20:14 Then Death and Hades were thrown into the pool of fire. (This pool of fire is the second death.)

20:15 Anyone whose name was not found written in the book of life was thrown into the pool of fire.

At this point the end time is presented as having two distinct aspects: the imprisonment of Satan (vv. 1–3) and the thousand-year reign of the just with Christ (vv. 4–6), all of this prior to the ultimate and definitive judgment that comes only at the end. Not unlike the moment of his first overthrow (12:7–9), Satan is thrown down, locked, and sealed, thus rendered completely impotent for a period of a thousand years. He is not yet eternally vanquished and will reappear briefly after the millennium. A thousand years *(v. 2): This is a figurative number. In Jewish thought, history was made up of a week of a thousand years, that is, 6 x 1,000. The Sabbath was the final day and it too had a millennium; it is this period that is being addressed.*

Why are there two resurrections envisioned (vv. 5,12) and two judgments? Two eschatologies are being combined here. First, there was the final period of the Messiah, an earthly reign of peace and justice. Then, in later Judaism, there was a final cosmic eschatology that went beyond the terrestrial character of the first. Thus, a segment of Judaism united the two and allowed for an extended period of time between them. New Testament eschatology allows for a period of time between the resurrection of Christ and the parousia, but there is no temporal breakdown other than that (1 Cor 15:20–28). This thousand-year period has been subjected to various interpretations, most of them literal. Some Western Fathers saw it as a period between the parousia and the general resurrection (Papias, Justin, Irenaeus, and Tertullian), with some Eastern Fathers (Clement of Alexandria, Origen) rejecting that interpretation. The most celebrated interpretation was that of Augustine, who simply saw it as the period of the church. A popular literalism saw the year A.D. *1000 as critical, either as the end of the millennium or as its beginning, all of which gave way to a sense of panic in certain quarters as the date drew near. Consistent with a contemporary interpretation of Revelation, we can best explain the millennium in symbolic or figurative terms as simply another way in which the book looks at the end time. It is but another layer or feature of John's eschatology.*

The reign of the just (vv. 4–6) *is concomitant with the capture of* Satan. Thrones of judgment (v. 4) *may be for the twenty-four elders or simply the twelve apostles (Mt 19:28). They reign to bring Christ fully to birth and are joined by all those who have witnessed to Christ during the early persecutions (v. 4). Martyrs have the place of honor in Revelation (6:9–11; 16:6; 18:27), and they are accorded participation in Christ's thousand-year reign. The remaining just must wait until the second resurrection takes place (v. 13). Those who form part of this first resurrection will have nothing to fear from the second when some of the resurrected will be consigned to eternal death (vv. 6,14). The just now enter upon their royal and priestly role previously mentioned (v. 6; 1:6; 5:10).*

The next image centers upon the release of Satan and the end of evil (vv. 7–10). Going forth from prison, Satan initiates his final onslaught. Gog and Magog *(v. 8): Originally a single eschatological figure, found in Ezekiel (cc. 18–19), Gog, king of Magog, has here become a "split personality." Satan enlists these two figures to move against the holy ones (v. 9). Symbolic Jerusalem is the beloved city (Ps 78:68; 87:2). Battle lines are drawn but there is no battle. Rather Satan (devil, serpent, dragon) is cast into the fiery abyss, to join the beast and the false prophet (19:20).*

The last image is that of the final judgment (vv. 11–14). This is universal in character and has cosmic dimensions. The judgment takes place before the Enthroned One, not identified as God or Christ, but at this point they have probably coalesced. With the judgment of each individual, history moves rapidly toward its conclusion. There are some scrolls pointing to a negative outcome, and one that is wholly positive, the book of life (v. 12; 3:5). Now with Satan gone and evil eliminated, death and the underworld (Hades) have lost their raison d'être *and so cease to exist (v. 14). The second death is final condemnation, and that is reserved for the unrepentant malefactors.*

THE ONGOING CONFLICT

"It was the best of times; it was the worst of times," as Dickens captured it, or if the language of today is preferred, "There is good news and bad news." Revelation speaks of a thousand years preceding the definitive defeat of Satan. The number is symbolic, but expressive of an era of relative peace during which time the power of Satan is not yet finally vanquished. Final victory is on the horizon but evil is still afoot. In the first Christian millennium many people took the number quite literally and lived in mortal dread of the number 1,000. As in so many instances in this book of the New Testament, the symbol leads us to another reality. The millennium can really be said to be the era in which we now live. With the resurrection of Christ, evil no longer has the upper hand; it has been chained and confined. Its defeat is real. But sin is still present and will remain so until the end. We stand between the "now" and the "not yet." Redeemed and baptized, we are confident of being on the winning side. And yet the struggle is not over. There is all too much ambiguity in our life. We want to remain faithful, fully confident of our final destiny, while we are honestly aware of the strong pull that sin has on us. The flesh and spirit struggle stands at the very center of our life.

Let's be honest. We love those moments of peace and tranquility when we know that things are right with God, and there is nothing we desire more than to remain in that strong realization that his love encompasses us. And yet the struggle remains. "The good that I want I do not and that which I want not that I do." There is always that shadow side: those times when our conduct is so much at odds with our stated beliefs. Do we not have those moments when we even have trouble identifying ourselves? There are those times when we walk a path that is totally irreconcilable with the calling that is ours. They are moments of shame, disbelief, and incredible guilt. It may take any number of forms, and it takes little soul-searching to discover the why and the how. But the fact is that the white mare has been transformed into the black stallion. And we wonder how God's love can ever reach us again. This is what it means to live in the millennium.

But if the life in God meant no struggle, what would be its worth? In every walk of life, there is sacrifice, and the more meaningful the prize, the greater the struggle. But there is the overwhelming truth that Christ has won the battle. As recipients of the Spirit and the motivation, victory is within our grasp. We do not have to fail. To choose sin is to choose the loser, the imprisoned Satan. His wiles may be appealing, but we have to wonder when we follow his lead.

To be on the side of Christ means to live a life that is coherent, one that makes sense, one that brings our values to bear. In those graced moments of peace we know that all is right with God. It may be in the silence of a dimly lit church, in the quiet time at the end of our day, at Eucharist or after the sacrament of reconciliation. Yet it is only through a constant return to our sense of purpose through prayer and self-denial that our spirit is strengthened and reinforced. We cannot expect the "afterglow" to continue without interruption. The world soon closes in on us and speaks values much at variance with what we profess. But it is only through developing a strong sense of purpose, a commitment to right over wrong, a desire to deepen our relationship with Christ living within us that we shall overcome. But to be on the side of Christ also means something else: to learn from our lapses. In the Christian life recovery is always possible. In fact it is within our grasp, if only the "fault" can become "the happy fault." It is at that moment of realizing our own human inadequacy in the pursuit of good and the importance of letting God make something out of our nothingness that life can be turned around. To turn our lives over to God is the path of holiness, and our weaknesses can make a vital contribution. It was not the religious authorities, so righteous in themselves, whom Jesus drew to himself; it was the tax collectors, the sinful woman, and those beset by demons.

THE SOCIAL DIMENSION

What is true of the individual believer is true of the broader community as well. During our "thousand years," we have seen all too many examples of good and evil on a large, even massive scale. More than one "evil empire" has come and gone in the past hundred years. But it is equally true that the discredited Satan still claims his followers. We continue to see corrupt governments that make the downtrodden grovel under oppression. Economic systems that thrive on profit continue to dehumanize workers and cause them to see their value solely in terms of productivity. Blatant forms of racism result in everything from exclusion and hatred to what is euphemistically termed "ethnic cleansing." The major holocaust of the twentieth century has been followed by other smaller but equally godless attempts to eliminate the unwanted. Societies that want to eliminate the unpleasant or the difficult frequently choose death over life, at its beginning or at its end, to solve the human equation. These and other issues are clear or subtle expressions of the continued presence of the vanquished evil one, who may be in his death throes but is determined not to go peacefully into that great beyond.

But the glass is also half-full! There are those many signs of life, which whether Christian or not, give evidence of the presence of God. War has been averted through conversation and a willingness to find solutions that do not spell human destruction. The United Nations finally has the possibility of becoming what it was originally intended to be: an international forum where the good of all humankind can be sought and solutions to problems can be pursued without resorting to arms. In following the dictum of Paul to "overcome evil with good," we see people who courageously put their lives and efforts on the line in the interests of the oppressed. Minorities, a word scarcely heard thirty years ago, have made us all more sensitive to racial, ethnic, gender, and sexual differences. We recognize the principle of equality, while admitting that we have not yet accomplished everything. Gains have come at a dear price for many people. But if there are ways in which we definitely see things differently today in the order of justice and peace, then the reign of God is among us. Much of the agenda, including environmental issues, remains unfinished, but we can still say that redemption continues to expand its horizons as a clear sign that the victory of Christ continues among us. A Catholic Church that could spread its wings and fly like a fledgling after Vatican II, a church that wanted to read the "signs of the times," that wanted to call members of other churches "brothers and sisters," that could speak of the promotion of justice as integral to evangelization bespeaks a presence of Christ in the world that was as unexpected as it was spiritually energizing.

How will Gog and Magog have their final day? None of us knows. Most of us will not be around, nor are we particularly concerned. But Revelation makes one thing clear. The *denouement* is not like that of a murder mystery; the outcome is already clear enough. Regardless of what turns and twists that history may take, it is God who will have the final word.

Millennium Thoughts

1. How do you understand eternal punishment?

2. Can you explain how we are already living in the millennium?

3. How do I experience the end-time struggle in my own life?

4. Are there signs of the triumph of Christ in the world today?

5. How do we reign with God as a "kingdom of Priests"?

THE NEW CREATION (21:1–22:5)

THE NEW HEAVEN AND THE NEW EARTH

21:1 **Then I saw a new heaven and a new earth. The former heaven and the former earth had passed away, and the sea was no more.**

21:2 **I also saw the holy city, a new Jerusalem, coming down out of heaven from God, prepared as a bride adorned for her husband.**

21:3 **I heard a loud voice from the throne saying, "Behold, God's dwelling is with the human race. He will dwell with them and they will be his people and God himself will always be with them [as their God].**

21:4 **He will wipe every tear from their eyes, and there shall be no more death or mourning, wailing or pain, [for] the old order has passed away."**

21:5 **The one who sat on the throne said, "Behold, I make all things new." Then he said, "Write these words down, for they are trustworthy and true."**

21:6 **He said to me, "They are accomplished. I [am] the Alpha and the Omega, the beginning and the end. To the thirsty I will give a gift from the spring of life-giving water.**

21:7 **The victor will inherit these gifts, and I shall be his God, and he will be my son.**

21:8 But as for cowards, the unfaithful, the depraved, murderers, the unchaste, sorcerers, idol-worshipers, and deceivers of every sort, their lot is in the burning pool of fire and sulfur, which is the second death."

THE NEW JERUSALEM

21:9 One of the seven angels who held the seven bowls filled with the seven last plagues came and said to me, "Come here. I will show you the bride, the wife of the Lamb."

21:10 He took me in spirit to a great, high mountain and showed me the holy city Jerusalem coming down out of heaven from God.

21:11 It gleamed with the splendor of God. Its radiance was like that of a precious stone, like jasper, clear as crystal.

21:12 It had a massive, high wall, with twelve gates where twelve angels were stationed and on which names were inscribed, [the names] of the twelve tribes of the Israelites.

21:13 There were three gates facing east, three north, three south, and three west.

21:14 The wall of the city had twelve courses of stones as its foundation, on which were inscribed the twelve names of the twelve apostles of the Lamb.

21:15 The one who spoke to me held a gold measuring rod to measure the city, its gates, and its wall.

21:16 The city was square, its length the same as [also] its width. He measured the city with the rod and found it fifteen hundred miles in length and width and height.

21:17 He also measured its wall: one hundred and forty-four cubits according to the standard unit of measurement the angel used.

21:18 The wall was constructed of jasper, while the city was pure gold, clear as glass.

21:19 The foundations of the city wall were decorated with every precious stone; the first course of stones was jasper, the second sapphire, the third chalcedony, the fourth emerald,

21:20 the fifth sardonyx, the sixth carnelian, the seventh chrysolite, the eighth beryl, the ninth topaz, the tenth chrysoprase, the eleventh hyacinth, and the twelfth amethyst.

21:21 The twelve gates were twelve pearls, each of the gates made from a single pearl; and the street of the city was of pure gold, transparent as glass.

21:22 I saw no temple in the city, for its temple is the Lord God almighty and the Lamb.

21:23 The city had no need of sun or moon to shine on it, for the glory of God gave it light, and its lamp was the Lamb.

21:24 The nations will walk by its light, and to it the kings of the earth will bring their treasure.

21:25 During the day its gates will never be shut, and there will be no night there.

21:26 The treasure and wealth of the nations will be brought there,

21:27 but nothing unclean will enter it, nor any [one] who does abominable things or tells lies. Only those will enter whose names are written in the Lamb's book of life.

22:1 Then the angel showed me the river of life-giving water, sparkling like crystal, flowing from the throne of God and of the Lamb

22:2 down the middle of its street. On either side of the river grew the tree of life that produces fruit twelve times a year, once each month; the leaves of the trees serve as medicine for the nations.

22:3 Nothing accursed will be found there anymore. The throne of God and of the Lamb will be in it, and his servants will worship him.

22:4 They will look upon his face, and his name will be on their foreheads.

22:5 Night will be no more, nor will they need light from lamp or sun, for the Lord God shall give them light, and they shall reign forever and ever.

In some of its most expressive symbolism, Revelation here presents the picture of the renewal of the universe and the Lord's taking up his dwelling among his people in the final era. The presentation is literary and not literal, and draws on a variety of biblical texts, many of which point specifically to the end time. Just as Babylon was representative of all that is evil, so Jerusalem, the holy city, becomes the symbol of all that is good. It is important to note that as the heavenly Jerusalem emerges, the historical, earthly Jerusalem lies in ruins.

Some of the operative texts:

- *The river of life (Ez 47)*

- *The end-time Jerusalem (Is 2:1–4; 65:17–25; Ps 46; 48; Heb 12:22; 13:14; Gal 4:24–31)*

- *Precious metals (Ex 25:5–14; Ez 28:11–17)*

- *Kings and open gates (Is 60:11–14)*

There are two visions: the descent of the new Jerusalem (vv. 1–8) and its description (vv. 9–27; 22:1–5).

The First Vision. *The whole of the cosmos is affected in this moment, which coincides with the final resurrection and the transformation of the world. With the new heavens and the new earth, everything connected with former times passes away and the new arrives (v. 1; Col 1; Rom 8:20–25).* The sea was no more (v. 1): *In Revelation, the sea is often identified with the presence of evil and chaos (13:1).* The holy city (v. 2): *The center of Jewish life, belief, and cult here becomes the symbol of the final presence of God to his people. The imagery of the city blends with that of Israel, the bride (Hos 2:16–22; Is 54:5–6 62:5; Ez 16:6–14; Eph 5; 1 Cor 11:2; Jn 3:24–30), as God and his people become one.* Dwelling with the human race (v. 3): *In contrast to the exclusiveness of earlier times (for example, Ez 44), in the new kingdom of God there is total openness. Both the symbolism and the language speak of the closeness between God and people, as the joy of the end time removes every semblance of sorrow (vv. 3–4).*

Yahweh enters the scene as judge (vv. 5–7), the one who is the beginning and the end (Alpha and Omega). Water *(v. 6): Final salvation is presented as life-giving water (Is 55:1), life in the Spirit (4:10–14; 7:37–38), a gift to the upright, to those who thirst (Mt 5:6). Here it is given to the victor, the one who has followed the Lamb, even under persecution. As the city represents both the presence of God and the dwelling place of the elect, God and the victor are spoken of as Father and son. Stronger than the expression of God and people, this looks to a true form of filiation rooted in God's Spirit (Gal 4:4–7; Rom 8:14–17). The separation from evildoers is now definitive, with the catalog of their sins drawn from vices common in the empire (v. 8).*

The Second Vision. *The messenger is an angel who has appeared previously. With the introduction of the Lamb, the new Jerusalem becomes his bride. The scene of the bride's descent is one of brilliance and transparency, the glistening of precious jewels (vv. 9–11). The twelve gates of the city, three facing in each direction of the compass, represent the twelve tribes of Israel (fulfillment; Ez 48:31–34) and the twelve foundation pieces, the twelve apostles, underscoring once again their singular role (vv. 12–14; Eph 2:19–20).*

The measurements of the city echo again the new Israel of Ezekiel (c. 40). The square city represents perfect harmony (vv. 13–21). Fifteen hundred miles in length, width, and height (v. 16): *Literally 12,000 furlongs. All the figures here are multiples of twelve. By ancient standards this would be monumental. It is sparkling and brilliant with all the precious stones known to antiquity. All of this reflects the otherness of God, expressed as a city that is one immense cube with the same dimensions on all sides.*

No temple (v. 22): *God is all in all (1 Cor 15:25–28). This is an abrupt departure from Jewish eschatology, wherein the renewal of the temple figured prominently. Since at this point God and his son are totally and immediately present to the people, there is no longer a need for sacred locales and space (Jn 4:21; Mt 18:20). Moreover, there is no longer any need for light-giving planets (v. 23). And the entrance of all people points to end-time universalism (v. 24). Hence, the new Jerusalem is a city renewed, God present, inclusive, bridal, beautiful, and holy; it is the new people of God.*

Flowing waters (22:1–5): *The life-giving river flows not from Ezekiel's temple (47:1–12), but from the throne of God and the Lamb (v. 1). Not only the water but all the symbols (trees, fruit, leaves) point to life in God.* Look upon his face (v. 4): *Forbidden to Moses (Ex 33:2–33) but now given to the elect as the reborn clean of heart (Mt 5:8; 2 Cor 3:18). This life is also light, the door to eternity and a perpetual reign, in the closing words that also end Handel's Hallelujah chorus (v. 5).*

THE CHURCH AND THE FINAL TIME

A scene of brilliance brings Revelation to a close. It is on a strong note of hope that the book concludes, as evil is finally vanquished and the forces of good triumph. In the language of a new heaven and a new earth, a wedding, and universal jubilation, the relationship between God and the world that came from his hands in the first pages of Genesis is set aright. In images that have deep biblical roots, evil fades from the scene, and God is "all in all."

The new Jerusalem that descends from above is two things: God's presence in the world and a redeemed people, the bride of the Lamb. That may seem slightly incongruous until we remember that such is exactly what the church is, a community of believers and the presence of Christ in the world. They are those who have washed their robes in the blood of the Lamb and have now reached their final destiny. We are those who are still on the journey. We are not yet totally redeemed. Indeed, we call ourselves a "pilgrim church."

Triumphalism is a state of mind within the church that fails to distinguish between the "now" and the "not yet." It may speak of individual Christians as sinners but never uses the term of the church itself. Regardless of where Christians may be on their pilgrimages, the church itself is holy and indefectible. She is already the heavenly Jerusalem, the bride spotless and unstained, who throughout history remains upright and transparent. And so one reads in church documents, as in the document on the Jewish Shoah, that the church calls her sons and daughters to repent of the evil for which they may have been responsible, but never is it said that the church herself repents. The reason lies in the fact that a church that is already perfect is in no need of repentance. Only her children are. And yet, on the other hand, we do not fail to see the holiness of the church's sons and daughters as the holiness of the church; it is the church's holiness that is seen through the sanctity of the members. The church as a whole is simply a magnified reflection of its members. Certainly it is a channel of life and grace; it is truly the body of Christ, and sanctity is of the essence. But the church is a mixture of flesh and spirit no less than any of its members. Each of us is a strange juxtaposition of the best and the worst. None of us is everything that he or she should be. Nor is the church. It is not yet the spotless bride, descending from on high, totally saved and sanctified. That day will come, as Revelation makes clear. In the meantime we are very much wayfarers, full of hope indeed, but a People of God making our way through the desert. This being the case, it is a church always in need of reform.

Because we know that the church is holy, its polarization in modern times presents a whole set of difficulties. For many it is "faith in a wintry set," a retrenchment that belies the forward-looking thinking of Vatican II. That the church has become more centralized in recent years and that strict orthodoxy has become the litmus test of advancement to church office can hardly be disavowed. The explanation of the achieved position is seen as the function of theology, and turning new turf is hardly applauded. There is a much higher level of frustration than authority in the church is wont to recognize, and it is all too debonairly dismissed as the voice of reactionaries. The church, we are told, was drifting away from its moorings and had to be restored. Many moderates suffer frustration because they see that much that was hopeful and promising is being dismantled.

Certainly there are people on the other side, those of a more conservative bent, who feel equally disenchanted. Their unhappiness extends from liturgy to catechetics and to unexpected turns taken in the life of religious communities. It would be wrong to think that these people are at home with the direction of the institutional church. Many of them are disappointed with that direction and alleged concessions they have seen take place; they would be quite happy to see a strong, more integralist government of the church.

And then there is the large silent majority, which sees itself as moderate. These are people who appreciate the tradition but have no great desire to be entrapped by it, people who welcome the future as much as they appreciate the past, and who are happy to see the possible become the actual in the reign of God. They will always be identified as Catholics and yet make their own decisions on many moral issues, especially those which are sexual in nature. There are many features of belief that they accept and defend. But they also demur. They see, for example, no reason why women cannot be accorded more recognition in the church (other than in official documents) or why celibacy must be seen as integral to the priestly state. And in the main their decisions on church leadership begin and end with their own pastor. "All politics is local" is as true for the church as it is for the state.

THE SPIRIT OF VATICAN II

We do not have a truly unified church, and on that point find ourselves at something of a distance from the end-time bride of Christ. Perhaps nothing makes concrete the entire issue more than the time-worn expression "the spirit of Vatican II." The more forward-looking face of the church looks at the steps taken to move the church forward in the past forty years as being done "in the spirit of the council," by which, as I have had occasion to mention, is generally meant a step not directly envisioned by the council but one very much in continuity with the direction that it espoused. A more traditional face of the church would say that such is an illicit inference. The council meant what it said and that only. For this reason we get opposing views on many issues facing the church today. The readiness the council showed to underscore the central role of the laity in the church is met with reactions that reinforce the importance of the clerical state. Efforts to broaden authority in the church by giving more responsibility for decision making to the local church are met with renewed efforts at the centralization of authority.

Now, as hard as it may be for some people to understand, there is a legitimate, even inevitable understanding of the "spirit of the council." The council did release a new understanding of the church and its role in the world; its principles proved to be elastic enough to go beyond their limited application at the time of the council. Just as a full understanding of a biblical text is not exhausted in a detailed understanding of its literal sense, so too the ultimate meaning of the texts of Vatican II is not limited to a repeated reference to the texts themselves. There was a spirit being captured in words at the council, and that is certain to continue to expand as the church's own self-understanding grows. This applies to many issues raised at the Council: the relationship among the Christian churches, Jewish–Christian relations, religious liberty, the understanding of the mystery of the church, to mention but a few. As difficult as it may be to believe at times, the winds of change are still abroad, and they will not be subdued. But disappointment is in store for those who in all good faith believed that the course of history would be changed in a single lifetime.

These issues simply illustrate why the bride of the Lamb remains a pilgrim, not one at her journey's end. The Book of Revelation enables us to take the broad view. The church does not begin and end within the period of our own life span. It has weathered many another storm, some of them more challenging than that of the moment. It has had a remarkable history and has made the face of Christ more visible in a dark and confused world. It has also been marred with sad and disappointing moments, which have made the human side of the church all too evident. And if we as a church are true to the spirit of Jesus, which vivifies us and points out our failures, then we as a church are not afraid to confess our sins and to ask for pardon.

The Acts of the Apostles tells us the amazing story of the early church's dealings with the question of the Jewish law. Were Gentile Christians to be burdened with the law once they entered the church? There were two schools of thought on the matter, each supported by rather strong personalities. Jewish Christians had strong feelings about the continued importance of the law and were quite opposed to its abandonment. Paul, with his

Gentile orientation, adamantly refused to place this burden upon the Gentile Christians. It proved to be a crisis of major proportions. On the outcome hinged the future of Christianity: Was it to be a full-fledged independent church or remain a latter-day Jewish sect? It made its decision in terms of freedom from the law, as related in summary form in Acts of the Apostles 15. The story has its own point. We cannot be held captive by the present moment; regardless of how elated or frustrated we may feel, the day will come inevitably when the bride will descend from the heavens as the new Jerusalem. It is a point on the horizon toward which we are still journeying. In the meantime we are still fed, nourished, and challenged by the voice of Christ in the church.

THERE WAS NO TEMPLE

Sacred space plays an important part in the Judeo-Christian tradition. From Jacob's designation of Bethel as a holy place to the tent built in the desert, and the twice-destroyed temple in Jerusalem, the presence of God in a determined place was part of Hebrew tradition. The New Testament takes a different turn. It has nothing of significance to say about a place of worship. Everything moves to a deeper sense of God's presence—in the individual believer, in the community, in sacrament. As the Jesus in John's Gospel tells the Samaritan woman, in the new dispensation there is no priority of place, or as Paul states it, we ourselves are the temple of the living God. It is little wonder that in the final Jerusalem there is no temple, just as there is no sun or moon. The light emanates totally from God and the Lamb, just as the all-encompassing presence of God in the believing community makes a place of cult an anachronism. It is at that point Paul tells us that even Christ is made subject as God becomes "all in all."

Of course, we shall always have places of worship. Many are great monuments to the faith of people. But they remain secondary in importance. In their sometimes sweeping grandeur, they take on greater significance than the people who worship there. But the cavernous cathedral has no more importance in itself than the simple mud-roofed chapel in a mission station. The main resting place of God remains the believer, and all of our

Christian ethic proceeds from there. It is human dignity and a Christian presence that measures all of our responses—life, respect, compassion. And from there the circle broadens in seeing all of God's human creation as sacred and worthy of our best. It is the brilliance of human goodness under God's grace that gives light to the new Jerusalem. The fact that we must walk in shadows now cannot dim the brightness of what is in store for a people of hope.

Looking at the Heavenly Bride

1. The final image is of a heavenly city. And yet many people have only negative feelings about the city and city life. How do we reconcile the differences?

2. Cosmic redemption stands at the end of the Bible, just as cosmic creation stands at its beginning. Do you see yourself as part of a universe being redeemed?

3. Discuss water as a biblical symbol.

4. In Revelation, God is the center and core of our life. How often do we reflect on the meaning of that?

5. What is the significance of the city without sun or moon? A city with open gates? A city with no temple?

6. Marriage, and therefore sexuality, is ennobled in the scriptures. Does our theology always reflect that?

IV. EPILOGUE (22:6–21)

22:6 And he said to me, "These words are trustworthy and true, and the Lord, the God of prophetic spirits, sent his angel to show his servants what must happen soon."

22:7 "Behold, I am coming soon." Blessed is the one who keeps the prophetic message of this book.

22:8 It is I, John, who heard and saw these things, and when I heard and saw them I fell down to worship at the feet of the angel who showed them to me.

22:9 But he said to me, "Don't! I am a fellow servant of yours and of your brothers the prophets and of those who keep the message of this book. Worship God."

22:10 Then he said to me, "Do not seal up the prophetic words of this book, for the appointed time is near.

22:11 Let the wicked still act wickedly, and the filthy still be filthy. The righteous must still do right, and the holy still be holy."

22:12 "Behold, I am coming soon. I bring with me the recompense I will give to each according to his deeds.

22:13 I am the Alpha and the Omega, the first and the last, the beginning and the end."

22:14 Blessed are they who wash their robes so as to have the right to the tree of life and enter the city through its gates.

22:15 Outside are the dogs, the sorcerers, the unchaste, the murderers, the idol-worshipers, and all who love and practice deceit.

22:16 "I, Jesus, sent my angel to give you this testimony for the churches. I am the root and offspring of David, the bright morning star."

22:17 The Spirit and the bride say, "Come." Let the hearer say, "Come." Let the one who thirsts come forward, and the one who wants it receive the gift of life-giving water.

22:18 I warn everyone who hears the prophetic words in this book: if anyone adds to them, God will add to him the plagues described in this book,

22:19 and if anyone takes away from the words in this prophetic book, God will take away his share in the tree of life and in the holy city described in this book.

22:20 The one who gives this testimony says, "Yes, I am coming soon." Amen! Come, Lord Jesus!

22:21 The grace of the Lord Jesus be with all.

The section reprises themes enunciated in the prologue (1:1–8). Christ is the central figure, as the purpose of the book is repeated and the authority of Jesus, "trustworthy and true" upheld once more. The angel was sent as a messenger (v. 6; 1:1); the heeding of the message's content is mandatory, with the return of the Lord a central belief (v. 7). Once again John falls in worship of the messenger (v. 8; 1:17), but such is excluded, with worship destined for God alone (v. 9).

Since the end is said to be imminent, the message is not to be sealed (v. 10). In affirming a repeated message of the book, final accounts are yet to be settled. Christ is the end-time judge, here applying to himself the Alpha–Omega title formerly reserved for Yahweh (v. 13; 1:8). Past images of salvation reappear: wash their robes *(7:14; 19:8),* tree of life *(22:2). Jesus is the davidic Messiah (5:5), and the source of resurrection (morning star) (v. 16; 2:28). Once again the churches are designated as the destinaries of the message (v. 16; 1:4).*

Marana tha (v. 20–21): *"Come, Our Lord." This was an Aramaic liturgical expression, used both to refer to the second coming and the eucharistic advent of the Lord. If the book were actually read in the liturgy, it would conclude before the central eucharistic action. Therefore the acclamation calling upon the Lord to come, would be followed by the assembly's response ("Amen. Come, Lord Jesus"), and conclude with the blessing, "The grace of the Lord be with all."*

Some Final Questions

1. What are my personal expectations for the future? My ecclesial expectations?

2. Do I appreciate the prolific use of symbols in Christianity?

3. How do I pray, "Come, Lord Jesus" *(Marana tha)*?

4. Do I truly appreciate the ugliness and destructive force of evil?

5. Do I truly believe in the final outcome? The full meaning of redemption?

6. Trees, water, light, and leaves—all speak of life in God. How have I experienced the power of these images in my own life?

7. What is the value of this biblical book in my life?

POSTSCRIPT

There are many people who find the Book of Revelation disconcerting, even a little appalling. War, bloodshed, beasts, and prostitutes do not constitute their idea of spiritual reading. Perhaps New Age thinking may find it a bit more palatable because of its jarring images, frightening contrasts, and a type of imagery that is not strange to contemporary stage productions and cinematography. The book has its greatest attraction in its use of biblical images, drawn from both Testaments, which leap out of every chapter in an almost endless array.

And what about the end time itself? Is all of this something that lies in the future? Something that humanity has to look forward to? The answer has to be in the negative if we consider New Testament eschatology as a whole. Let's return to the example that was presented in our introduction and view it more in detail. The Book of Daniel is the most likely candidate for first place in apocalyptic literature. Written during the pagan hellenization of Palestine in the second century B.C., it predicts the advent of God's reign with imagery as striking as any found in Revelation.

Hence it is particularly striking that the Gospel of Luke clearly sees the fulfillment of Daniel in the advent and mission of Jesus. A simple illustration proves the point. In announcing the birth of John to Zechariah (1:10–22), the angel Gabriel appears in the temple at the time of prayer, with Zechariah himself praying. The latter registers fear at the vision, with the former commenting, "I was sent to speak to you" (Lk 1:19), and urging calm and freedom from fear. After the message, Zechariah becomes mute as a "sign." All of these same features are present in Daniel 9–10, with the sole biblical appearance of Gabriel (Dn 9:20–21), Daniel praying in distress (9:20), in fear (8:17; 10:7), reassured (10:11), the "Fear not" (10:12), and finally the visionary being struck mute (10:15).

Luke clearly wants to see the Book of Daniel's hopes realized in the coming of Jesus the Messiah, with the early church seeing itself as the end-time community. Therefore, as Christians of the third millennium, the first thing that we must realize is that we are already living in the "final period." Evil still wages war; the dragon, the beast, and the great prostitute continue to seek their prey, to weaken all of us and deter us from grasping the great vision. Who can deny it? When we consider the human tragedy that surrounds us in the modern examples of attempted geno-cide, the ruthless conduct of uncaring governments, the violence in our communities and in our homes, the lack of moral concern in modern media—all speak very clearly the message of evil. But there is also the immense good that surrounds us in the examples of dedicated peacemakers, a United Nations that has begun to take steps as a genuine catalyst for good and conflict-resolution, elected officials who have a vision of the common good, churches and other agencies who witness strongly to the power of good. And then there are those witnesses to holiness whom we meet every day of our lives.

The end of Revelation clearly echoes its beginning. There is the figure of John, prostrate in worship, the angel presented as the message bearer for the churches, the enthroned God and the Lamb. Beyond that, the last book of the Bible carries us back to the first. We have the Genesis tree of life, the abundant waters that nourish it, and the light that casts out all darkness. The biblical narrative has reached its end. God's design for humanity, which has moved from sin and alienation to total restoration, has been set forth in its entirety. For the grateful soul there remains only the final plea: Come, Lord Jesus.

In our commentary we have recognized the temporal inaccuracy of the early church's thought. The return of Christ was initially seen as being close at hand. But we can understand the rationale that undergirds that belief: Christ as the Lord of history and the convergence of all of history in Christ and God. Regardless of what twists and turns human events may take, the final word belongs to God. This is truly fundamental for the person of faith. We have also considered what might be called the anticipated parousia, those sudden and unexpected inbreakings of God into history that result in dramatic shifts in our lives and our thinking. Further considerations looked at our personal parousia, those direct encounters with God that will come when our lives run their course.

As we have said, the tension of New Testament eschatology between the "now" and the "not yet" reminds us that we truly live in a state of redemption. Salvation has been achieved, even if it is not yet finalized. We are a people who see in faith the glory of God shining in the face of Christ. In Word and sacrament, we live in a state of vibrant hope. The major part of redemption is already achieved, and so, with Paul we ask, "If God has gone this far on our behalf, will he not bring us home as well?" In Genesis the sun and moon dispelled the darkness, which was identified with evil and chaos. We too live in the sun, with a vision that is real even if incomplete, and at times sight is "through a glass darkly." But sight it is, even if at times we are all too matter-of-fact about it. To reflect on the fact that God who spoke to us in sundry ways in times past through the prophets and sages has now spoken to us in his Son, the definitive Word never to be matched or repeated, gives us inestimable sight. It is this vision that led martyrs to their death, missionaries to distant lands, ascetics to surrender everything, and theologians to plumb its depths. Life is anything but purposeless. Because of the vision of faith, we have sacrificed to educate our children to appreciate its meaning and to pattern their lives on what they have learned. The major milestones of our lives are centered around our faith: from birth to death, in Word and sacrament, we are accompanied on our journey.

For the ancient peoples, water and life were synonymous. And it is the theme of water that wends its way through the entire biblical narrative, reaching its climax in the "living water" of John's Gospel. And that symbol means that we have both the vision and the means to realize it. The water of Christ is the gift of the Spirit, which bonds us with God, unites us intimately with Christ, and springs up to eternal life. Hence, for those who live in the Spirit, death has already taken place in baptism and the passage to eternal life is simply a transition. It is the Spirit that makes acceptance of the Christian message possible; without it we could never say, "Jesus is Lord." The Spirit is the water that gives growth to the tree of life.

THE REIGN OF GOD IN SOCIAL ISSUES

The reign of God, as we have had occasion to note, is the era of God's sovereignty over all of creation. The church is the beacon that points to it, and within the church many of its elements are present. But the reign of God is not coextensive with the church; it is larger and broader than church. We yearn for the reign's fullness while realizing that its presence is incremental. The reign of God becomes more apparent with every step taken in fashioning a more just, respectful, and habitable world. The struggle for justice and equity on this planet is clearly a reign-of-God issue. Think of the dogged determination of people who dedicate themselves to unpopular causes for years at a time, some for gospel reasons, others simply because they believe it is right. One thinks of nuclear testing sites where people have gathered for years, especially during Holy Week, to pray in protest for an end to such tests. Or those who have continued to protest, even to the point of civil disobedience, at an American military facility where military personnel from other countries are taught the tactics of brutal repression to quiet opposing voices in their countries. Or the courageous example of people opposed to the death penalty, abortion, or assisted suicide, who continue to raise their voices in support of life.

A faith stance embraces both a personal and social morality. To eliminate the threat of war, to work for respect for the environment, to eliminate the marginalization of minorities is simply to realize that "the heavens and the earth are his, and all that is contained therein."

A wide chasm separates the believer and the nonbeliever, and it is not easy to come to a common understanding. Many people of no particular faith see the importance of doing good solely on humanist grounds. They may well believe that a moral code has only a relative value. For such people, to speak of history as God-directed is absurd, and to speak of the end of history in

Revelation's terms makes no sense at all. The perspective of a person of faith is sharply different. The existence of God shapes the outlook and the comportment of the believer at every turn. The person of faith is willing to wrestle with the inconsistencies in the presence of evil in light of the broader vision. And yet the believer and agnostic can come together around a variety of concerns that afford a common ground. They stand together under the common title of "people of good will," the people whom John XXIII included as destinaries of one of his early encyclical letters. We have long spent time enumerating our divisions; the day has come to see and appreciate the many concerns that bind us together. For many wounds in our society today we can join together in binding and healing.

The last book of the Bible is as baffling to some as it is compelling to others. It is noteworthy (and consoling) that even in matters of the Bible there is room for a diversity in taste. This book is strange to some because it is an apocalypse, an unveiling of God's relation to the universe in surrealist symbolism that can be both appealing and appalling. But it deals with real and fundamental features of human existence, the struggle between good and evil that has dogged creation and every individual within it from the dawn of history. It brings Christ to the apogee of his New Testament presentation. He has triumphed over sin and death, and he now reigns with the Ancient One. The suffering of the elect, those who have finished the course, has vanished. In that picture of the final time, that day yet to come, that final page still to be written, the sovereignty of God is universal. It is a gathering of people of every tribe and nation in uninterrupted glory, when every tear will be wiped away. It is for this that we yearn with every fiber of our being. Come, Lord Jesus! Come!

SELECTED BIBLIOGRAPHY

Beasley-Murray, G. *The Book of Revelation*. London: Oliphant, 1974.

Boring, M. E. *Revelation*. Atlanta: John Knox Press, 1989.

Caird, George. *A Commentary on the Revelation of St. John the Divine*. New York: Harper, 1966.

Cerfaux, L. *L'Apocalypse de St. Jean*. Paris: du Cerf, 1964.

Collins, Adela. *The Apocalypse*. Wilmington: Glazier, 1979.

Court, John. *Revelation*. Sheffield (Eng.): JSOT Press, 1994.

Feuillet, A. *L'Apocalypse, etat de la question*. Bruge: Desclee, 1963.

Fiorenza, Elizabeth. *Revelation: Vision of a Just World*. Philadelphia: Fortress, 1991.

Giblin, C. R. *The Book of Revelation*. Collegeville: Liturgical Press, 1991.

Glasson, T. F. *The Revelation of John*. Cambridge: Cambridge University Press, 1962.

Harrington, W. T. *Revelation*. Collegeville: Liturgical Press, 1993.

Johnson, Alan. *Revelation*. Grand Rapids: Zondervan, 1983.

Kealy, Sean P. *The Apocalypse of John*. Wilmington: Glazier, 1987.

Laws, Sophie. *In the Light of the Lamb*. Wilmington: Glazier, 1988.

Metzger, Bruce. *Breaking the Code*. Nashville: Abingdon, 1993.

Minear, Paul. *I Saw a New Earth*. Washington, D.C.: Corpus Books, 1968.

Mounce, Robert. *The Book of Revelation*. Grand Rapids: Eerdmans, 1997.

Perkins, Pheme. *The Book of Revelation*. Collegeville: Liturgical Press, 1983.

Prevost, Jean P. *How to Read the Apocalypse*. New York: Crossroads, 1993.

Roloff, Jurgen. *Revelation*. Philadelphia: Fortress, 1993.
Sweet, John. *Revelation*. London: SCM Press, 1979.
Thompson, Leonard L. *The Book of Revelation*. New York: Oxford University Press, 1998.

TOPICAL INDEX